A Hero's Journey.

Year Six

The Awakening

N A Kesaris

Ann Ellen O'Neill
You taught me about love, hate, forgiveness
and everything inbetween.

Thanks for being my mum.

ISBN: 978-1-9822-8451-0 (sc)
ISBN: 978-1-9822-8453-4 (hc)
ISBN: 978-1-9822-8452-7 (e)

Disclaimer:

All swear words within this text have been altered to protect any adults who may stumble across its pages. They can be such delicate, easily offended flowers – who roll their eyes, whilst spouting tripe which begins with 'In my day....'

Let's not add to their misery.

Hello.

?	Narrator	Bit daft, eager to learn. Loves a chat. Been 'Here' before...
	Vinnie	11 years old. Fed up with school and family life. Some anger issues.
	The Orb	Quite bright in colour and in wisdom. On a mission to save Vinnie.
	Egolian	Small angry spikey ball of negativity, massive anger issues.
	Cat of extraordinary floof	Bit of a menace, may also have anger issues.
	Mum	Loves her family, likes to run. Can be a bit bonkers.

	Dad	Loves his family and football. King of dad jokes.
	Ben	Vinnie's little brother, general good boy, a pain in Vinnie's backside.
	Mrs Teague	Headmistress of the school, means well, heart in the right place, can also be a bit of a battle axe when needs to.
	Alfie	Best friend of Vinne, loves football, online gaming and wotsits.
	Helen	Year six teaching assistant has trouble smiling. Should have considered a career change years ago.
	Mr Winterbottom	Newly qualified teacher. Bit like Marmite, you either love him or hate him. Vinnie not a fan.
	Nan	Loves Vinnie and Ben. Often babysits, enjoys boardgames and watching sports. Quite glamourous.

Sunday.

> *'All our dreams can come true,*
> *if we have the courage to pursue them.'*
>   - Walt Disney

Hello? Hello... You there. Yes, YOU. The **Reader of the words**,

Do you know *why we are here*? I *sense* that I may *have* been in this **place** many years

ago. But it **looks** so *quite different* now. I find **myself** here. With *you*.

Not that I am *upset* of course, for you *do seem* very nice!

Perhaps the **twisted hand of fate** has *thrown* us **together** in this manner

for a **good** *reason*.

Reader, do *you see?*

Do you see **where** we find ourselves this springtime evening?

I fear that there *may be little* of interest for **us** here.

we are in front of a *rather* **uninspiring** house of 3 bedrooms located somewhere

on the **island of mud**.

I **believe** it to be known as *England*.

The **eve is late**, the **day is winding down** to a close.

Let us take a *closer look* inside, we may find CluES as to *why we are here*.

No, no, no *do not worry* dear **Reader**, we **shall** not be *seen* by any

inhabitants for we are *merely observers*.

Let us **enter** through the *front door* and SEE what **we** shall *come upon*.

Careful Reader, for it, is a tad **grubby**.

Ah, it has led **us** into a **small** *hallway*.

Reader, tell *me*, what is that *fusty smell* about the *air?*

I assume that its origins are **indicative** of SOME sort of *foodstuff*, perhaps

devoured earlier on *in this eve*.

Huh?! You **believe** it to be the *fingers of fish?*

One does learn new things every day for I had **not a clue of clues** that *fish even had fingers*.

Well, well, well my interest has been **piqued**.

Let's **investigate** this place a little more, if we are **lucky** we *may see* some of these *fish with fingers* for **ourselves**.

I see a **further** white door.   let us **peek** inside.

Oh, it leads us into a **small** sitting room.

Reader see, over there, it **appears** *to be* two *adult humans*.

Oh, you know of this.   A **mum** and **dad** you *say?*

Yes, yes now **you** *mention* it, I do recall, I **encountered** such a thing before.

They **do not seem** interesting, this 'Mum and Dad' for they **stare** mindlessly at a **small window** within their **hands.**

Heeding **no attention** to the larger window, which shows two **adults** getting **angry** with each other, *shouting, crying* and generally being **queens of the drama**.

A phone? A TV?

I **do not** recall those curious items the *last* time I visited this place.

How **unusual**.

Reader, the **energy** of this room reaches out for us like *a long bony hand of boredom*.

Let's venture *further along* the hallway.

Oooh look a warm **cosy kitchen**. The pungent smell of the *fishy fingers* is **stronger** here.

Its only *inhabitant* is a *cat of* extraordinary *floof* snoozing soundly.

Can you **hear it** purring?

I can **see** its **dreams**; it is dreaming of the time the family **tried** to **fob** it off with **cheap** kitty food. So, it **pooped** on the hallway rug in the early hours of the morning. One of the adults **stepped into it** with **no slippers** on.

This **memory** makes the cat **purr more loudly** and it str—et—ch—es itself full length.

Not much *else* to **see** here, time to *leave* the floofy **pampered** cat.

Come now **Reader** and *follow me up* this narrow **dark** staircase.

Upon the **landing**, we can **see** that the *only light* comes from **a bedroom** at the **front** of the **house**.

At the **back** of the house, are **more doors**, *hmmmm*, this first room is *closed*.

A **sign** on the door reads **'Ben's Room'**.

I *wonder* what a **'Ben'** is.

It is most **definitely** *a living creature* for I hear it breathing, soft *shallow* breathing suggesting *it is at rest.*

Let's leave **'Ben'** be.

We should **move** towards the **lit** room.

A sign on the **door** suggests a **'Vinnie'** resides here. The door is *slightly* **ajar**. allowing **us** to venture **inside**.

Our eyes rest upon a male.

He is not quite a child and not quite an adult.

He is of that age I believe adults often refer to as 'awkward'.

The room is in darkness, except for the glare of another TV.

The light from it reflects on the boy's face

causing him to look slightly demented and unusual.

His *teeth* are **bared** and gritted. He is immersed entirely within the

game.　　　　He is *playing 'online'*: you say?

Competing against others and it is life or death?

He must be the last player standing?

The concentration on his face and the scowl on his mouth suggests that he

may not be doing so well.

Reader let us *stay awhile* and OBSERVE this CREATURE for

I feel in my water.

we maybe just in time for a little excitement.

"Oh, get lost, that's not faiiiiirrrrrrr. gaaarerrhhhhhh the game must be gliiiiiiiitched!!"

Vinnie screams and shouts at the game, getting more and more stressed. His eyes bulging out of their socket's, spittle flying from his mouth as he hurls insults at the television screen until he cannot take it anymore.

Whhhiiiiizzzz

The game controller flies through the air.

Crash!

Shattering into fragmented pieces of plastic as it hits the wall across the room.

A blinding white light shoots out of it lighting up the entire room.

Vinnie pushes himself along his bed, shielding his eyes from the glare, he blinks a few times and pats the seat of his trousers just to double-check he didn't poop his pants. The light dissipates, in its place, a bright shining orb of orange hovers above the shattered remnants of the controller. Vinnie squeezes his eyes closed, rubs them with the backs of his hands and opens his eyes again.

"What...... Whattttt..... the........... actual??"

Stammering, unable to comprehend what he sees before him.

Vinnie begins to wonder if his mum was somehow right and too much time on Edgebox games really has messed his head up.

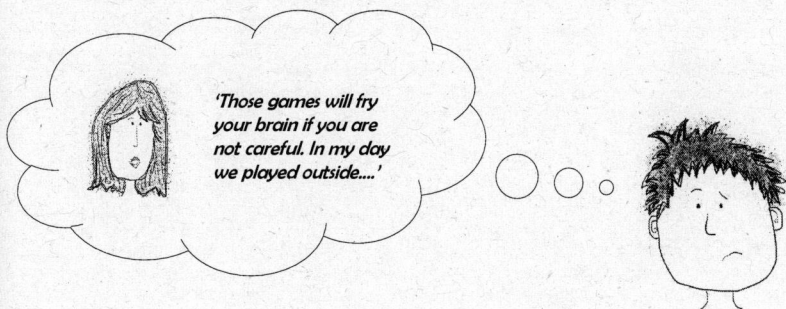

Lost in thought, he jumps with shock when the bright light talks to him.

"Do not fear me, Hero,

for I am your Essence."

The Orb speaks in soft gentle tones.

Immediately bringing calmness into the room and into the boy cowering upon his bed.

Sitting upright Vinnie leans towards The Orb of orange which is now moving slowly towards him.

The Orb hovers just in front of Vinnies's face casting a dim yellow shadow as it settles.

"You're me what now?"

The startled boy's voice has returned to normal, all quivering and stammering gone, his questioning is calm and curious.

Vinnie stares into The Orb, its translucent nature allowing him to see through it, he raises a hand to touch it; stopping abruptly as The Orb speaks again.

"I am the part of you where forgotten dreams and desires lurk, I am you before Egolian took over and banished me from you. Think back to a time when you were younger, and you felt invincible when you could be and do whatever your heart desired.

I am that."

Fear creeps ever so slightly back into his Vinnie's voice.

"Ego what now?"

The strange Orb explains further.

"Egolian is in you. When you have an opportunity for a new experience or a new idea – it is the voice that 'talks' you out of it.

The Egolian is not equipped to make decisions about your life's journey, for it is like a small child".

Vinnie's eyes widen, the quivering returning to his voice.

"In Me? IN... ME?"

The Orbs calm tones once again fill the room.

"Hero, go and look in that mirror, I will show you."

Vinnie moves tentatively towards the edge of the bed, taking care not to whack The Orb with his bottom as he stands up.

He walks slowly towards the mirror which is across the other side room. As he does The Orb shines its light on it.

The image in the mirror causes Vinnie to fall back slightly, eyes full of fear.

Staring back at him is a small almost fluffy looking creature. Its hair is spikey and red, its eyes yellow and its mouth jagged and angry. In fact, its whole expression is angry and uncomfortable.

Turning his head towards his bedroom door Vinnie begins to stammer.

"mummmm, mummmm......mummmmmeeee..."

The Orb directs Vinnie back to the bed with its light.

"Oh you, sausage of silliness, no one else can pacify the Egolian inside of you. Not even your mummy! Sit back down and I shall explain."

Sitting back down on the bed, Vinnie is not listening to The Orb at all. His mind wanders as he begins to mutter to himself.

"How did the Egowatchamathingy get in me?
I bet it was that burger my aunt made for me last week,
it did taste very odd..."

The Orb suddenly turns a funny red colour, and it speaks a little louder than it had been at the distracted boy on the bed.

"It is AN EGOLIAN!!"

This unexpected change in volume does indeed bring Vinnie's attention back into the room and The Orb continues.

"It has always been in you.

It is made up of all those times you have felt scared, anxious, worried, or angry. It is all those times people have told you that you are not able to do something. Those adults who label you as shy, naughty or a pain in their backside.

Those times you felt stupid or not good enough.

It is all those knots in your stomach when you have to stand up in front of the class or do something you have never done before.

Its job is to keep you safe, but its only idea of keeping you safe is to avoid anything it regards as new or different."

Vinnie's thoughts wander again. He looks down at his tummy.

"Hmmmm......
I wonder if I could just poop it out.."

This causes The Orb to change colour again as it responds clearly exasperated.

"Oh, my days!! Heroes don't **POOP** out their Egolians!!

They **MASTER** them."

Vinnie responds, quickly deciding that he does not want to upset the strange orb hovering in his bedroom any more than necessary, for he is still none the wiser as to what it actually is and is a bit worried it may decide to join the angry red dude inside of him.

"Okay okay — I'm listening! What does the Egosamalamadingdongthingy want?"

The Orb explains.

"The EGOLIAN wants to keep you in the Comfort Zone.

A desolate place where nothing new or exciting happens and where people lose their Essence Orb, sometimes forever."

The threat of being lost forever weighs heavy on The Orb.

"Well, how do I get it out of me?
I don't want to be a house for an Egotrassid".

The Orb floats close to Vinnie, stopping to hover about an inch from the end of the boy's nose. Vinnie starts to get an itch on his nose, he wiggles it slightly to ensure the sneeze does not escape for if it was to erupt from his nostrils it would propel The Orb through the window covered in sneezy snot.

Vinnie is not sure that would be well received.

The tickling in his nose thankfully subsides as The Orb continues.

"Heroes cannot remove their Egolians, it seems some cannot even say it correctly.

Hero's must pacify them so that they may escape the confines of the 'comfort zone'. Here is a note pad, I will teach you the tools you need. "

The Orb magically summons a rather plain black covered notepad and a pack of pens into the room.

Vinnie looks at it aghast, suddenly brave, he confronts The Orb.

"Hang on a mo. I'm gonna need to *write* stuff down? Can't you just tell me while I play another game of Twice weekly on the Edgebox?"

The Orbs voice is tinged with desperation as it responds.

"Hero, Hero, Hero if you are to pacify your Egolian, you will need to trust me and do exactly as I say, or else you could be lost forever."

It must help the boy or The Orb itself will be gone into the abyss of lost hopes and dreams forever.

"And anyway, how are you to play with a broken controller?"

This last comment causes Vinnie to suddenly spring into action.

"Darn it, forgot about that.
I'll be right back.
I just need to ask my mum summink......"

Leaving the room before The Orb has a chance to protest.

Moments later the sound of muffled voices floats up the stairs.

The Orb strains to listen, the voices become a little louder as though a disagreement is occurring.

Sudden silence shortly followed by a sound, similar to that of a toddler in a supermarket who has been told no to a lollypop, appears to be emanating from the stairwell, it gets closer and closer until....

...Vinnie is back in the bedroom.

His face blotchy from angry emotions and frustration.

"Muuuuummmm says she won't buy me a new controller. it's so unfaaaaaiiiiiiiir. my other friends have more than one controller. mum says coz I have broken two of them I have to wait till my birthday. It's SOOOO UNFAAIIIIIIIIRRRRRRRR."

Vinnie plops down on the bed no longer caring that The Orb is even in the room or the Egolian in him. He sits there, fists clenched, lips thin and eyes half-closed silently brooding about his perceived bad luck.

The Egolian inside of him is smiling to itself feeling confident that this particular boy will be no trouble at all to keep in the comfort zone.

It doesn't notice The Orb float nearby.

The Orb's light glows brighter, warming the boy's face as it manifests itself into a pair of headphones and plops on to Vinnie's head.

Almost instantly, Vinnie visibly begins to calm down. He giggles slightly, his breathing becomes relaxed, and his shoulders soften. After a short while The Orb transforms back into its natural form and floats once again near Vinnie.

Vinnies's face is now aglow with curiosity as he turns to The Orb.

"what was that?
One minute I wanted to trash my room
    and hated my mum and now..."

The Orb, whose glow has now returned to its normal brightness, explains.

"This is what I am going to teach you, Hero. This and many other ways to tame the Egolian inside of you. For it is that which creates and then feeds off your emotions. It thrives on your loss of control."

Vinnie reaches down and picks up the notebook, this time with no whinging about having to write stuff down.

Pausing, he looks at The Orb.

"Before we start though, why do you keep calling me Hero?"

The Orb hovers close, its warm glow permeating the very air as it proudly explains.

"Ah, that is easy.

You and every human on the planet have the potential to be Heroes. You, my boy, has the makings of a great Hero.

Follow my instructions and you will see exactly what I mean.

Now first things first, say Eeeee-go-liiiiii-aaaaa-n."

Vinnie tries and tries to get his tongue around the word.

"Egofartin......"

 "..erm Egolion......"

".... Erm......."

He stops for a moment, then all of a sudden his eyes light up as though the most amazing of ideas had just sprung into his puzzling head.

"Oh, blast .... I'm just gonna call it **Brenda**. Yeah, Brenda will do."

The Orb is confused.

"Why Brenda? I don't understand."

"Well, I figured,
it won't be so scary if I call it Brenda."

He shivers ever so slightly as he remembers the image in the mirror.

But a big smile soon stretches across his face.

"I mean, who has ever been scared of a Brenda!"

The Orb cannot argue with such logic.

"What a splendid idea Hero!

By calling it Brenda you are indeed removing some of its power over you. For it feeds upon your fears. Well done!

Hero write that down in your notebook."

As Vinnie writes in his book he stops for a moment.

"Hey, Orbster, what is this weird square thing that has just appeared in my notebook? Hang on a mo, there are three of them!!"

The Orb explains.

"The one with the television set is a short film all about someone who has managed to master their own Egolian and gone after what they want."

Vinnie peers at the small television which appeared in his book.

"But how will I see the film?"

"You must use the force Hero........."

Vinnie glances at The Orb.

"Huh?!"

"Oh erm, No sorry. I meant the phone.

You must use your phone Hero.

Scan the QR Codes with the camera or app,

and the material will play."

Vinnie shakes his head.
Questioning if this Orb is all that smart after all,
before returning his attention to the notebook.

"The headphones one is there to help you when you are feeling cross and cannot calm down.

Pop your own headphones on. Close your eyes and listen.

Allow it to calm you down so that you may think clearly."

A small smile spreads across Vinnie's lips as he continues to jot down the words of wisdom emanating from The Orb.

"The last one is a gift from me, a little something to make you smile.

Smiling and laughing instantly helps us to lift our mood and create positivity.

Have you ever noticed that when you smile at people they cannot help but smile back?"

The Orb looks over as Vinnie finishes writing in his notebook.

Vinnie lets out a sneaky yawn.

"Well done Hero, that is an excellent start to your journey.

But now is the time to rest. We have some busy times ahead of us."

At that very moment, Vinnie's mum calls upstairs.

"Vin.... Get ready for bed, I'll be up in a minute to tuck you in..."

Usually, Vinnie would complain but not tonight for It has indeed been an evening of the most unusual kind and he is very ready for bed.

Vinnie puts his pad and pen on the floor next to his bed.

After some rummaging under the crumpled duvet and squashed pillows on his bed, Vinnie finds his Pyjamas.

Swiftly removing his tracksuit bottoms and t-shirt and rolling them up into a ball shape, Vinnie lobs them across the room. Narrowly missing The Orb they fly past it and land in a crumpled heap on the floor next to the laundry basket.

Mum's voice once again floats up the stairs.

"Don't forget to brush your teeth...."

Pyjamas now on, Vinnie mooches out of the room.

Meanwhile, The Orb has settled on top of the wardrobe where it feels it would be safe from any more flying clothes as judging by the mess on the bedroom floor the wardrobe is rarely used for storing any clothes.

A quick brush of his teeth, and Vinnie is back in the room. He settles himself under the warmth of the duvet.

Soon after footsteps can be heard coming up stairs, as mum comes it to put him to bed. She kisses him gently on the forehead, all thoughts of the earlier argument forgotten.

"Good night Vin......
.... sleep tight".

Vinnie is already half asleep as mum switches off the light and heads back downstairs.

Letting rip with a silent sleepy parp under the covers, Vinnie drifts off and is soon snoring softly.

Well **Reader of the words!** What did I say, I knew something interesting was going to *happen!!* I knew it! My water is very rarely **wrong!**

Oooooh, I'm **so excited**, I feel a **rhyme coming on**.

An ordinary boy we did see,
Get super stressed and proper angry.
He broke the controller for his game,
And cannot play, oh what a shame!

There was a flash of light so bold,
It left behind an orb of gold.
"Save us", it speaks in a calming tone,
Before we are lost to the 'comfort zone'.

The magic squares, like the boy was shown,
Will give **you** the things upon **your** phone.
Point the camera, a beep will be made,
Then the magic in the squares can be played.

So, reader, let's not stand and stare,
I see the notebook over there.
Have a peek and you will find,
There is also great power within **YOUR** mind.

Find the Egolian within

<u>Stand in front of a mirror.</u>

Then you should <u>imagine</u> <u>what</u> <u>your</u> Egolian looks like........

eeek!

Brenda

That way, when the '<u>voice</u>' <u>tries to talk you out of</u> doing something it has a '<u>face</u>'.

It may help to give it a <u>non-</u> scary name, like <u>Nigel</u> or <u>Dave</u>.

Egolian is the voice which tries to talk You out of stuff which although may seem a bit scary will ultimately bring you closer to your goals.

The voice you hear when you are thinking about doing something which may harm you is your common sense and should always be listened to.

Monday.

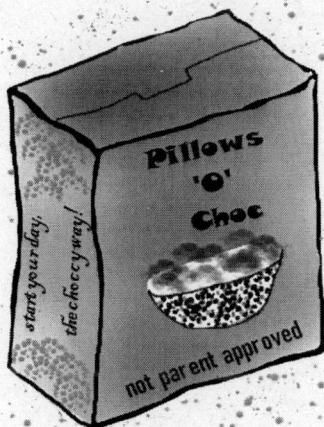

start your day, the choccy way!

Pillows
'O'
Choc

not parent approved

A good morning of mornings to you **dear Reader**. That **Disney** chap was a **busy fella**.

Fancy being told that he had *'no good ideas and lacked imagination!'*

Good job **he chose** to **believe in himself** instead of listening to such **codswallop**, hey!

Let's go back in and **see** how **our Hero** is after **his shock** yesterday.

The sun has started to **rise**, and **the house** is beginning to **stir**.

Incidentally, **I** have **decided** to **name my Egolian 'Norman'**.

When I **looked in the mirror** to see **'Norman'** he looked like a **wiggly little worm**, quite **different** to 'Brenda'.

How does *yours look?*

Oh. *How interesting* for it would seem that **no two Egolian are the same**.

Hmmmmmm I **wonder** if that is because **no two lives are the same**.

I mean, **we all** have a **different experience** and **perception of the world**.

Anyway, **upstairs** we **must go**. Back to the **bedroom**.

CAREFUL READER, you nearly *stepped on* the floofy cat hiding *on the*

top step, that would have *been* disastrous for you. For it will surely have

clawed *your* very toes to the death.

The bedroom door is slightly ajar, in we go. Oooooh, there is our Hero.

He sleeps so soundly. I shall take a peek at his dreams.

Oh, that is odd, for no dreams are happening here. It is like an empty void; no sound can be

heard. I suspect dear Reader, that Brenda has stolen them. The situation must be

serious indeed.

Surely he must wake soon, the day is itching to get underway.

"....... Vinnnnnnnnnnnieeeeeeeee......."

Gaaaaaaaaaahhhh!!

My goodness Reader that sudden intrusion made me jump, our *Hero's* mum has a decent *pair of lungs* upon her, for her shouting almost *deafened me.*

Oh, **hoorah!** I see the covers moving.

Our Hero awakes.

Vinnie stuffs his head under the pillow and within seconds the only sounds to be heard are soft shallow breathing and the odd squeaky fart coming from the sleeping boy under the duvet.

A few minutes pass until..........

".......Vin Get UPPP......."

Mum hollers up the stairs again, her words tinged with obvious frustration at the sleepy boy's lack of movement.

A muffled sound emanates from under the covers *'leemeeelooone'* it seems to mumble.

A few minutes of silence pass, the boy is in slumber once again.

The floofy cat wanders into the room sniffing the air.

Looking for somewhere to rest it's floofy face.

"....VIN GET UP....

or I will whip that duvet off ya!"

Mum's angry expression suddenly pokes around the door, ensuring that Vinnie fully understands he has now run out of options. The last time he ignored mum at this stage she did indeed walk in and whip the duvet off Vinnie, leaving him cold and shivering on the bed.

The floofy cat is startled by this sudden noisy intrusion.

Jumping high in the air, its tail and body taking on the appearance of a toilet brush, as it runs from the room.

This added commotion and the prospect of lying cold on the bed, spurs Vinnie into action.

"Alright, Alright I'm flipping up now."

He shouts at both mum and the floofy felon, as he flings back his nice warm covers.

Wandering from the room in a zombie type daze, stopping only to scratch his backside through his pyjamas and fart loudly Vinnie slowly mooches along the hallway.

Enters the bathroom he sits on the toilet resting his weary head in his hands.

Suddenly a chirpy happy voice appears in the bathroom as The Orb flies in through the closed door.

"Gooooood Morning Hero!"

It catches Vinnie completely by surprising causing him to let out a strangled scream.

"Gaaaahhhhh!"

Managing to cover his modesty with one hand, and with surprisingly quick reflexes for such a sleepy fella, Vinnie steadies himself on the toilet seat with the other.

If he hadn't he would have most definitely have fallen face-first onto the cold floor tiles with his pyjama bottoms around his ankles and his bum in the air!

A shocked Vinnie turns to The Orb.

"Flippady Doo Dahs, I thought you had been a dream bought on by eating too much cheese on my baked beans last night!"

The Orb replies in a sprightly manner.

"Oh no Hero, I am indeed real.
and what a beautiful day it is outsi......"

The Orb falters, its orange glow turning slightly green.

"Hero, quick, leave this place for evil lurks.
I sense its' stench....."

Vinnie is now fully awake and none too impressed.

"Oh, for goodness' sake, seriously Orby thingy.
It's just my morning poo.
Privacy Please!!
                    Jeez....."

Vinnie waves his hand towards The Orb in an attempt to waft it back through the door, he succeeds only in wafting his stench full pelt into The Orb.

The Orb disappears at speed through the closed bathroom door, and back into the safety of the bedroom.

A good twenty minutes later the bedroom door opens, Vinnie wanders back in, yawning absentmindedly.

Letting out an almighty shout as he stubs his toe on the side of the bed.

"OUUUUUCH!!!!"

Plonking down on the bed Vinnie clutches his foot and rubs his big toe like mad.

The Orb reappears, its orange glow returned.

"Hero, as I was saying. It is a wonderous day of opportunity!"

The pain from the early intrusion still etched upon Vinnie's face.

"Must you be so chirpy? It is barely 8am."

He asks still rubbing his big toe.

"Ah, well. Here lies your second lesson.
Grab your pen and we shall begin".

The Orb is super keen to get this Hero up to speed and mastering the Egolian within him as quickly as possible.

Vinnie. Not. So Much.

"Not bliddy likely! I'm starving!!"

With that, Vinnie disappears from the room making his way downstairs to grab some breakfast.

He walks too quickly down the stairs which causes him to lose his footing, he slips as he reaches the last four steps and bounces down them on his bottom like a demented kangaroo.
He makes his way into the kitchen rubbing his left butt cheek.

Now safely in the kitchen he takes his cereal from the cupboard.
It is a hideously sweet offering of chocolate filled pillows with the nutritional
value of an actual pillowcase. He hungrily opens the box to discover it has
only 3 pillows of cereal left in the bag. His mum walks in to find him staring
in disbelief at the empty box.

"Muuuuuum"

He begins to whine.

"Mummmmmm. Ben has eaten all the cereal again.
He is soooo annoying. Now, what AM I TO EAT?"

Vinnie's mum, who has overslept slightly and not had her coffee yet, is in no
mood for this.

"Well Vin if you got up earlier you would have had the last bowl.
Ya snooze, ya lose.
Remember the early bird gets the worm n all that."

Vinnie stares at his mum, confused thoughts whizzing around his head.

Worms? Birds?

What on earth is she whittering on about??

I only wanted the blimmin cereal.

It is just further proof that she loves that little annoying bratasauras more than **me**.

Why is she not telling that annoying little brat of a brother off for eating all the cereal?

Realising mum has stopped talking and has returned to making her coffee. He begins again.

'Well, what am I going to eat? *Muuuuuummmm??*'

The last word was said with an extra helping of whine, just to make sure she knew just how peed off he is with the situation. Vinnie stands by the cupboard with his arms crossed trying to look as fed up with the cereal situation as he can.

He *always* has that cereal; he can feel a tight knot in his stomach at the thought of having to have something different.

It is 'Brenda'.

At this very moment, it is manifesting feelings of frustration and 'unfairness' in Vinnie.

Even small changes can cause the Egolian to manifest itself as a negative emotion.

Vinnies's mum, on the other hand, is shuffling around the kitchen in her fluffy slippers, talking baby talk to the cat and ignoring him.

*" Who is mummy's precious angel?
You are, awwww, yes you are......"*

Vinnie tries again.

"Muuuuuuuuummmmmmmmmmmmm."

This time with extra, **extra** added whine and a scrunched up look on his face.

"Oh, for goodness' sake Vin.
There are other cereals in the cupboard have one of those.
I don't have time for this nonsense."

Vinnie looks in the cupboard again but all he can see is 'healthy' cereal, the one that looks like it will taste of cardboard.
He tries once more.

"But... Muuuuuuuuummmmm........."

She cuts him off mid whine using her 'nearly cross but not quite' mum voice.

"Vinnie... Have what's there.
You are going to be late otherwise.
If you are late you will get into trouble again.
NOW HURRY UP."

With the kitchen now bathed in silence, mum turns and leaves clutching her much needed cup of coffee.

Vinnie is alone once again.

Even the cat had grown bored of the show and darted out of the cat flap, it is now staring randomly at a plant in the garden.

With a heavy, hungry sigh, Vinnie grabs the 'healthy' cereal and pours some in a bowl.

He misses it slightly and some cereal ends up on the floor, crunching under his feet as he walks to the fridge for the milk.

As he adds the milk, some splashes on the countertop.

He stares at it for a split second, then ignoring it, sits at the table to eat.

Spooning some into his hungry mouth he chews slowly.

Hmmmm..
Well, this isn't so bad.

With added enthusiasm, Vinnie grabs a larger spoon of cereal and milk.

This time, however, he misses his mouth, and it ends up all over the lap of his pyjamas.

Whilst the disastrous breakfast is taking place in the kitchen, The Orb is having a bit of a nosey parker moment in the bedroom.

It has disappeared under the bed and does not notice Vinnie re-entering the room and begin putting his school uniform on.

Vinnie is still brooding about the breakfast fiasco, his voice tinged with irritation as he confronts The Orb.

"Er, orby thingy, what on earth are you doing?"

The Orb comes out from under the bed coughing and spluttering with a smelly old sock stuck to it.
It shakes the sock, but it does not come off.

The Orb shakes itself harder and harder until.....

..........the sock flings off, whizzes across the room

and whacks the unsuspecting boy right in his eye.

"Hey, watch it!"

Vinnie rubs his eye as he plonks back down on his bed already worn out from the morning's events.

The Orb is still in slight shock from it's under the bed ordeal.

"Perhaps our next lesson should involve a vacuum cleaner."

Vinnie lets out a loud and dramatic,

"Yawwwwwwwwwwwwwwwwwn."

at this most ridiculous of suggestions.

"Anyway, Enough of this time-wasting!
Hero, I must teach you more of the tools
you need to master the Egolian inside of you
before it is too late.

Grab the note pad."

Instructing the disgruntled boy as The Orb explains further.

"This universe is made up of energy and vibrations......"

The Orb is interrupted by Vinnie sniggering loudly.

As Vinnie sniggers a small slimy bogey flings out of his nostril and hangs there momentarily as though it has just committed an adrenaline-filled bungee jump.

Vinnie wipes it away on the back of his hand and straight onto the crumpled bedsheets beneath him.

"Well, that's a load of rooooobish for a start!"

exclaims Vinnie.

"Vibrations and energy? ....
I mean come ON Orb."

"Hero, Hero. Do not mock me for it is true.
It has been a truth since the dawn of time."

The Orb glows a warm yellow as it tries to explain.

"Well, Orby thingy, we have never been taught that in school.
And I have been in school for a long time. Year 6 now you know.

That means I know practically everything there is to know about everything."

Vinnie retorts, still sniggering slightly at The Orbs apparent stupidity.

"And I know that the universe is made up of planets, rocks, water and lots of space."

The Orb continues, despite Vinnie's obvious reluctance.

"Let's use this morning as an example. What happened when your mum woke you up?"

Vinnie scratches at some dried milk on his chin as he casts his mind back.

"Well......"

"She shouted up the stairs.."

" ......which woke me up a bit..."

"So, I put the pillow on my head and went back to sleep for a bit."

The Orb takes this opportunity while Vinnie is giggling at the memory to ask a question.

"Then did you get up?"

Vinnie rolls his eyes at The Orb, clearly irritated by the seemingly simple question as he responds.

"Well, no. You know I didn't!! Mum stuck her head round the door all angry with me. Then I got up."

Unperturbed by the eye-rolling, The Orb presses Vinnie further.

"How did you feel when you finally got up?"

Vinnie ponders the question for a split second, before continuing.

"Hmmmmmmmm, well I was really cross
that I had to get out of my bed;
it was so warm and cosy.
This wasn't helped by you scaring me
whilst I was having a poo..."

The Orb hastily interrupts Vinnie, not wishing to dwell too long on that memory.

"Ahem, yes, well, ignoring that. What happened after?"

"I stubbed my blimmin toe on the bed then I nearly fell
down the stairs trying to get away from you."

Vinnie carries on recalling the events of the morning barely stopping for breath as he does.

"Then my stupid brother had eaten
all my favourite cereal then mum got cross
because I didn't want the other healthy rubbish
then the stupid cereal fell in
my lap making my pyjama bottoms all milky
then you flicked a sock in my eye and now this......"

Vinnie shoves his foot at The Orb, his big toe poking through a large hole in his sock.

The Orb winces as it declares:

"Hero, you created all of that misfortune this morning."

"Did not."

"Yeah, you did."

"Did not, did not, Did not"

"Yep, all of it".

"Diiiiiiiiid not not not not not!"

"Hero, I will explain....."

The Orb continues quickly before Vinnie can chuck another 'Did not' at it.

"As I was saying. The universe is made up of energy, vibrations, and laws.

All types of laws.
Some are created by man to keep order and people safe. For example, if you kill someone you have broken a law and will spend time in prison or even the death sentence depending on where in the world you committed the crime. Some are laws which we have no control over like the rotation of the earth around the sun and the gravitational pull of the earth."

Vinnie yawns loudly whilst picking at the now drying bogey on the bedsheets, causing The Orb to stop.

"I thought you were going to tell me stuff I DIDN'T know; all this is taught in schools already!"

The Orb continues, trying to remain focused on the conversation and not be distracted by the sight of Vinnie now rolling the bogey between two fingers and then flicking it at the TV screen.

"Well. In addition to those more well-known laws are some others.

One of those is the 'Law of Vibration'.

Put simply, positive thoughts and actions attract more positive things and negative thoughts, and actions attract more negative things.

Understanding this law will open your mind to the 'Law of Attraction' but we will talk about that one another time.
These laws are the most powerful tools you can use to master the Egolian inside you."

Vinnies's interest is reignited as he remembers the angry little red thing inside him, as he does his tummy knots slightly.

"So, tell me Orby McOrbface,
how come I have never heard
of this so-called 'law' before then?"

This question causes The Orb to glow once again a little brighter as it responds.

"Hero, I am pleased you have asked. It is excellent to want more information, it shows intelligence.
There are some things we can do to 'prove' the power of the Law of Vibration, and once we have, I believe you will then trust in the power of the universe and your own self to shape your life".

Vinnie beams at this compliment,
often when he questions the teachers at school
he gets told off for 'back chatting'.

The Orb carries on, full of optimism from the smile that it sees across Vinnie's face.

"Many people believe that they are not in control of what happens to them.

Mistakenly believing that it is the external elements of their lives which direct their life paths."

The Orb explains further.

"The 'Law of Vibration' suggests that it is simply not true.

Yes, the things that happen in your life do have an impact on you, BUT you have a CHOICE about how much they affect you and what you choose to FOCUS on.

YOU have the power within to create the life YOU truly want."

Vinnie is looking at The Orb, but his attention has wandered slightly.

Concentrating for periods of time has always been a struggle for Vinnie, (Whose mum suggests he has the attention span of a mosquito).

I wonder if I can just fix the controller myself.

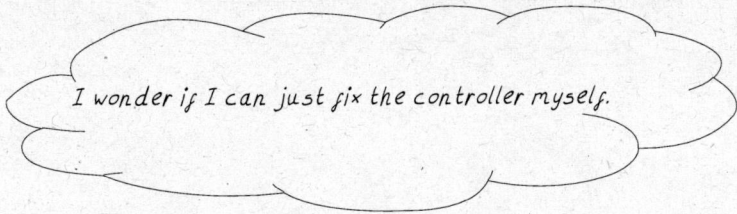

Completely unaware that Vinnie is lost in thought The Orb continues its teachings.

"There are 5 simple things you can do in the morning to help create positive thoughts and with it, positive things."

The Orb moves the note pad and pen towards Vinnie.

"I call it The Power of 5."

The motion of the notepad being pushed by an invisible force across the bed brings Vinnie back to the conversation.

"Huh?!"

"Hero, I said there are 5 simple things you can do to start creating the positive vibes needed to attract more positive vibes and with it the power to master the Egolian inside of you."

The Orb continues to push the notepad up to Vinnie's leg and nudges him with it a few times until Vinnie eventually picks it up.

As The Orb speaks, Vinnie writes.

"Number 1.
Set your alarm clock without a snooze function.
Giving at least one hour before you need to leave for school. Then...."

As The Orb mentions the 'S' word, Vinnie suddenly springs into life.

"SCHOOOOOL!!"

Vinnie can hear the muffled voices of mum and Ben at the bottom of the stairs and realises that they are getting ready to go. Mum will call up for him any minute and be super cross if he is not ready.

"I have got to go!!"

Vinnie drops the pad and pen on the bed and grabs his school bag.

The Orb begins to leave the bedroom with him.

"No way! You can't come!
My friends will think I'm nuts."

Vinnie closes the door abruptly behind him, heading downstairs just as mum turns to shout up the stairs.

"Oh, hi Vin, was just about to call you. Let's go..."

Luckily for Vinnie they only live a five-minute walk from the school and as Vinnie is now in year 6, mum doesn't mind him making his own way to school.

This also suits Vinnie as it means he doesn't have to walk with his little brother.

With a muffled 'bye' Vinnie whizzes past mum and Ben and legs it up the road towards the school.

Well **Reader**. I don't know about **you,** but that *hectic morning* made me spin a little dizzy!!

Our **Hero** could *use his poop* as some sort of **superweapon**.

That poor **Orb** may be scarred *forever* from its stinky **encounter** in the

bathroom.

I think the **journey** ahead may be a *tad bumpy* for this **Hero**.

Oh, my *days*, my *mornings*, my *years* I'm so **intrigued** my **rhyme is on**........

Morning is here and the Hero awoke,
His morning was beyond a joke.
Mum called for him to wake,
Three loud times this did take!

He shuffled sleepily to the loo,
The orange orb disturbed his poo.
Brenda must be loving the show,
Especially when he whacked his toe!

what bad luck, but it did not end there,
He nearly fell all down the stairs.
A spoon of cold cereal in his lap,
It made him such a moody chap.

The notes he wrote are not complete,
He left for school, quick on his feet.
The Orb was left behind ignored,
I bet it will spend the day quite bored.

But Reader, not us, let's go,
I want to keep watching the show.
Quick, jump up, oh don't whine,
We have to get to 'school' on time!

The power of five

1. Set the alarm clock. At least **one hour** before you leave for school

Monday
continues.

Come on, be fast **Reader**! Our Hero *acts quickly* when he **needs to**, *Wheeeeeeee!!*

How *exhilarating* to be in the **fresh air**, do you *feel it* on your *face* as **we run?** We are **lucky**

that it is **not raining** just now, for I **have heard** that **England** is quite often **wet and soggy**.

The **breath** is coming *fast from your lungs* as *our pace quickens*, you *feel* and *hear* your

feet hitting the **pavement**. The *vibrations* of every step *whizzing up your legs* –

it is an *amazing* feeling **Reader**; you *must agree* this **running malarky** makes one feel

ALIVE!

Our Hero is about to *turn a corner*. We **must not** lose sight of him for I have *not the*

cluest of clues what a **'school'** even is and would not know **where to look for one**.

Of course, of course. *How silly of me!* **You** would know, you are indeed a very **clever**

Reader, I must **not** underestimate you!

There he is. **Look**. Just *up ahead*. His pace has **slowed**.

As **our Hero** walks I *see* he is being joined by **other** young humans. I see **boys** and **girls** are

moving in the same direction. **Reader**, I am a *little confused*. Do **all** the young humans of

England dress *exactly the same*, for **all** the *boys and girls* are **wearing** the same top?

A **uni-form** you *say*, I am **enjoying** this **adventure**; I am **learning new things** every minute! What purpose, **Reader**, does a **'Form of Uni'** *serve?*

It **shows** which **school one attends?** Does *this mean* there *is more than one?* How **exciting!**

Well, how curious **Reader**. Who is *that person* who **stands** within the **centre of the road?** It **appears** to be an *adult human woman*, dressed head to foot in *brightly coloured yellow.*

A **'Lady of Lollipops'?**

Why on *earth* would she need such a **big 'lollipop'?**

Is it to hit the **children** on the **bottom** as they pass if they are **late** for **'school'?** No?

Oh, that is a *shame* for that *would have* been **fun** to **see!!**

Look, our **Hero** has crossed the road near the **'Lady of Lollipops'** and is now *entering* a **large iron gate.**

Mrs Teague, the headmistress, addresses a group of children and herds them towards the school playground as though they were lost sheep.

"Quick, Quick, Children for you are almost late."

Forcing a smile as she does for the benefit of any parents who may still be nearby.

Vinnie turns to his friend Alfie, rolling his eyes slightly as he responds in irritated tones, just loud enough for Alfie to hear.

"Almost late?
So, she basically means
we are on time then?!"

His friend sniggers whilst nervously checking Mrs Teague had not heard.

Vinnie and Alfie enter the school playground just as the lining up whistle is being blasted out by a rather short stout woman with curly hair and a chin wart which seems to do a little dance whenever she speaks.

Her face etched with a weariness one can only assume has come from too many years spent herding children about the school.

FWEEEEEEEEEEEETTT.....

At the sound of the whistle, all the children on the playground automatically get into lines behind each of the teaching assistants.

They are then walked purposefully into the school and towards their classrooms.

Vinnie and Alfie joined the year six lines. Their classroom is at the top of the school on the first floor.

The children chat with each other as they move through the corridor ignoring the adults as they shout:

'be quiet',

        'stop pushing each other'

                and

                    'who has lost this cheese and pickle sandwich?'

The jostling begins to dissipate as the children enter the classroom and sit at their tables.

Vinnie is sitting somewhat towards the back of the classroom, still chatting to Alfie when the class teacher Mr Winterbottom, (who is in his first year as a teacher and often looks like could do with a hairbrush, a good night's sleep, and a suit two sizes smaller) walks in and demands quiet.

"Alright, Alright. Settle down."

Vinnie does not hear the class teacher for he is too engrossed in telling his friend about the broken Edgebox controller.

He woefully informs his friend that he will not be able to play Twice Weekly later.

"It just exploded into
like a gazillion pieces......"

The conversation is suddenly halted by a very loud, barking interruption.

"You there.
Yes YOU, the one who thinks the calls for quiet do not apply to
him. I do not expect to have to wait for YOU to have finished
YOUR conversation before I can get on with MY day.
We have lots to do."

This causes both Vinnie and Alfie to momentarily take on the facial
expressions of a couple of startled guinea pigs.

Vinnie attempts to explain that he just hadn't noticed the teacher enter the
room.

"But Mr Winter..."

The teacher is in no mood to listen.

"DO NOT ANSWER ME BACK, I do NOT have time for this. That will be a strike. It is NOT even 9am."

Mr Winterbottom has clearly had a bad morning too; his patience is non-existent as he roars at Vinnie with the same vigour as a hungry bear just out of hibernation.

The other children in the room smile nervously at their classmate's bad luck to be caught in the grumpy teacher's radar and decide that they shall keep out of Mr Winterbottom's glare as much as they can.

At the mention of a strike Helen, the teaching assistant, gets up and saunters over to a board where all the names of the children are in view.

She places a black mark next to Vinnie's name thus compounding the misery of his morning further still.

Sitting there, brooding Vinnie can feel the injustice of the situation wriggle inside him like a coiled angry snake.

Why didn't Mr WinterBUTThole let me explain?
I wasn't being rude.
I just didn't hear him.

Mr Winterbottom is now taking the class register.

Vinnie's head, on the other hand, is busy with thoughts of unfairnesses. The black mark against his name on the wall seems to burn right into his skull every time he looks at it.

Suddenly the entire class rises and begins to head silently to the door.

There is a school assembly that morning.

The whole school must listen to the headteacher reading a story.
She must choose them from 'The Big Book of Boring Stories'.

It bores the pants off an entire hall of children and teaching staff on a weekly basis.

Vinnie's classes sit on the benches, a privilege given to the year 6 students as it is their final year.

Just as Vinnie joins the line, Mr Winterbottom calls out.

He motions for Vinnie to move to the end of the line whilst jabbing his pointing finger in Vinnie's direction.

"NOT YOU.
YOU can sit on the floor today.
YOU cannot be trusted not to talk during the assembly."

Vinnie moves slowly past the other children to the end of the line, frustration and anger continue to bubble inside Vinnie as he catches some of the other children giggling at his misfortune.

Brenda is loving the show.

Thoughts and feelings in Vinnie's head are a jumbled angry mess.

....Not fair.... ....justwantcontroller...: ....hateschool......
.... mumlovesbrothermorethanme.....

Unable to hide the irritation; Vinnie's mouth is set in a thin line and his shoulders are hunched as he walks down the corridor and into the hall.

Vinnie is made to sit on the floor near their class teaching assistant.

The headteacher soon settles into her flow and rattles off her boring story to a hall full of kids. The children move and twitch on the floor as though they are sitting on a nest of ants.

Vinnie glances around the room.

He catches sight of a teaching assistant across the room attempting to hide an almighty yawn with her hand. His gaze rests upon another couple of assistants, these two are having a whispered chat at the back of the hall.

Tapping the kid next to him Vinnie tries to show him the chatting assistants but as he does so Helen jabs his shoulder with her finger whilst giving him THE look.

Vinnie glares at her before looking down at the floor.

The boring story has ended, and the assembly is now focusing on kids whose birthdays are coming up that week. They are summoned to the front of the hall and a couple of the year six's must navigate their way through the hall, past Vinnie.

Vinnie is once again lost in thought.

He is clenching his fists tightly as the negative feelings literally take over his entire being.

Brenda, is replaying all the annoying things that have happened to Vinnie over the last few hours.

As one year six child walks past Vinnie to join the birthday children at the front, Vinnie sticks his foot out slightly, causing the child to almost trip.

Helen glares at Vinnie again.

This will most certainly be another black strike against his name.

Vinnie doesn't even know why he stuck his foot out, it just kind of happened and this adds to his internal angry vibes.

The assembly comes to a close and the children shuffle out of the hall.

It is the summer term which is the last term of school before the children break up for the holidays and thus reach the end of whatever school year they are currently in. For Vinnie, this will mean the end of his time at Primary school and a whole new school awaits him for September.

All the year 6 teachers are about to do various assessments on the children to understand where they are regarding the learning they have done throughout the year.

The children all feel the pressure to get the questions right as test results go to their new schools.

The teachers feel the pressure to prove they have taught the children correctly.

The school has a somewhat electric, nervous feeling about the air which is not normally present.

Back in the classroom, Vinnie is not surprised to see the Helen go straight up to Mr Winterbottom to tell him of the events in assembly.

The injustice of it all continuing to fill his mind space.

Bet she doesn't mention the chatting teaching assistants at the back of the hall.

As the children are all quietly looking towards the front, Mr Winterbottom decides to confront Vinnie about the assembly.

Using it as an opportunity to show off his authority to the other children in case they too have any rebellious thoughts.

Vinnie feels his face go hot as Mr Winterbottom begins.

"Vinnie, I am *extremely DISAPPOINTED* to hear that you were unable to focus on the assembly even though you sat next to Helen.
                    This is a further strike against your name.
We are coming up to SAT's week and we need to make sure everyone is giving their BEST EFFORTS and that Vinnie, includes YOU."

Mr Winterbottom starts the English lesson, he is reading the final chapter of a book called 'Tom's Midnight Garden', about some sort of time travelling clock thingy.

Vinnie tries hard to listen as he knows tomorrow they are going to have to do their own stories.
The teacher finishes the book and after a short discussion with the class about the ending, it is break time.

The day continues, maths, lunch, and yet another strike against Vinnie's name for apparent backchat later, it is finally time for home.

Three strikes in one day gives Brenda power inside him, the Egolian is bathing in the negative energy.

Vinnie is quickly out of the school gates and on the short walk home. Mum no longer waits for him when she collects Ben as Vinnie is allowed to walk home alone.

Sometimes he may head to the park next door to the school to kick a ball around with his friends, but not today.

Today his mind is on other things.

Vinnie's pace quickens as a tiny spark of fresh hope causes him to decide to take a look at the broken controller.

He intends to try and fix it himself he really wants to lose himself in a game of Twice Weekly with his fellow gamers.

The Orb is napping on top of the bed when Vinnie gets home and back to his bedroom.

"Where the bliddy hell did I leave it?"

Vinnie mumbles to himself as he starts to lift up scattered clothes from his bedroom floor to peek underneath them.

In no time at all, he spots the smashed controller, clearly broken beyond repair.

"Oh, Maaaaaannnn....."

His current gaming predicament and his mother's voice refusing to replace it echo around his head.

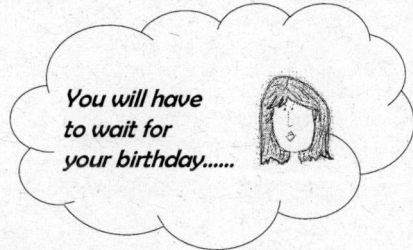

You will have to wait for your birthday......

The rage bubbles up inside him, he cannot control it.

The backpack is the first thing to fly across the room.

It hits the wall and slumps to the ground.

Vinnie's rage continues.
Kicking the dirty clothes littering his floor around the room as though they were deflated footballs.

His breath is fast and shallow.

His pulse quickens and his heartbeats loudly within his chest.

His palms are sweaty, and he is so enraged that he appears to be completely unaware that he is even in his bedroom.

Brenda is bouncing around inside him with glee at this turn of events.

Vinnie launches a well-aimed kick at his pile of dirty washing and in doing so, a pair of underpants with an iffy brown skid mark on them fly up and land upon the now stirring Orb.

The realisation of what is on it hits The Orb like a pungent punch to the face.

"Ewwwwwwww!!"

It lets out a high-pitched shriek as the pants ping off and land upon the ceiling light shade, where they hang swinging back and forth for a few moments before plopping to the floor.

"Hero, Hero..........."

The Orb tries to get Vinnie's attention.

But the boy is so fired up with rage that he cannot hear The Orb.
The Orb floats closer, careful not to join the underpants on the ceiling fan.

Transforming into headphones, and settling on Vinnie's head, just like before.

A calmness enters the room.

Vinnie's breathing begins to return to normal and he flops onto his crumpled bed with tears of exhaustion and frustration slipping down his sweaty red face.

Allowing Vinnie a few moments to collect his thoughts The Orb transforms back and speaks to the boy.

"Hero. Talk to me. Tell me what is wrong."

The Orb's voice is soft and soothing, Vinnie looks up at it.

"No different to any other day
            at that smelly bog of a school.
Mr WinterBUTThole is constantly talking about how
important SAT's are and how we must try our hardest."

Vinnie allows all his frustrations to cascade out of his mouth like a woeful waterfall of words.

"I have been trying hard all through that school.
Ever since year one, all my teachers keep telling
my mum and dad is that I need to concentrate more.

            Concentrate, concentrate!!!

I just don't get it, I thought I was CONCENTRATING..."

He takes a breath before continuing.

"And another thing the stupid teaching assistant Helen just keeps telling everyone how HARD high school will be and that I am in for a 'shock'.

Whatever the hell that means!"

Vinnie stops for a moment as his angry outburst has caused his nose to leak, he has a drip of runny snot about to make its way down his lip.
Looking down, he finds a t-shirt poking out from under his foot.
He wipes the snot from his face on it and lobs it back onto the floor.

"And to top it off. I can't even play my game because my STUPID MUM WON'T REPLACE MY CONTROLLER!"

With this last outburst, Vinnie turns and shoves his face into the crumpled bed covers.

"Hero, I feel your frustration.
But, by letting these emotions rule your head,
you are allowing Brenda to grow stronger."

The Orb's attempt to communicate is met with a wall of stony silence from Vinnie, whose head is still buried in the bedding.

The Orb sighs slightly but continues on regardless.

"Brenda is making you feel knotted inside.

The Egolian enjoys it when emotion takes over for it fogs the way out of the Comfort Zone – for you see nothing, you observe nothing.

The emotional feeling is *all you are focusing on.*"

The Orb stops as there is a muffled noise coming from the bedcovers, Vinnie's face is still wedged in them.

"Gmupphhhy nod no li dis"

"Hero, to be heard you must sit up,
        it's no good burying your face in the bed."

Vinnie sits slowly up, his face red and blotchy, partly from the anger outburst and partly from the lack of oxygen received when trying to breathe through a duvet.

"I said I do not like feeling like this."

He repeats his words whilst wiping his nose on the back of his hand.

"But everything is SO UNFAIR!! I do nothing wrong ever...
Everyone just HATES me.
            It's not my fault."

Vinnie swings his body around ready to launch himself back into the duvet.

But this time he is caught mid-air by an invisible force.

                        The force is coming from The Orb.

It has suspended the whiney boy about a centimetre from the bed.

The top half of Vinnie's body is twisted slightly.

"waaa wwaaaa waaaa??!!"

Vinnie stammers, the only parts of his body he can move are his lips and his eyes.

"What have you done to me??"

The Orb hovers close to Vinnie's face.

"I felt it necessary to freeze you in the moment.

I want you to concentrate only on this moment.

And to be completely honest,
I am fed up having a conversation with your bottom."

Still hovering close to Vinnie's face, The Orb continues.

"In school today, do you remember how cross you were with Mr Winterbottom?

Think back and remember how the feelings of anger filled your every cell.

YOU CHOSE TO LET the angry emotion take hold and by doing so,
YOU ALLOWED the Egolian inside of you to take control."

The Orb stops briefly to allow this information to register with Vinnie, before continuing.

"Do you want me to share with you how you can use the 'Law of Vibration'
        I mentioned to you this morning?
                You do remember our conversation from this morning??"

The Orb had to ask, for it is not entirely sure how much of the Hero's brain was in proper working order earlier that day.

Vinnie tries to nod his head to acknowledge that he did, forgetting he was frozen, he sees The Orb still waiting for a response, so he mutters.

"Yeah, yeah I s'pose so.
But I don't get it.
Sounds like a load of rubbish to me."

        "If I unfreeze you, do you promise to sit up and listen?
        NO more bum in the air, crying into the duvet business?"

Vinnie wastes no time in responding.

"Yeah, ok. But just so you know I wasn't crying!"

As soon as this reply is out of his mouth Vinnie unfreezes and lands back on the bed with a bounce. He sits straight up in fear of The Orb freezing him again.

It was not a very pleasant experience.

"Marvellous, that is good news!"

The Orbs glow has brightened slightly now that Vinnie is giving it his full attention.

"Now, grab your pen and write this down."

The Orb waits while Vinnie searches on the floor of his room for the pad and pen.

The room looks like it has been ransacked by a gang of blind pirates, so it takes Vinnie a good few minutes to locate them.

Once he has he plonks his bottom back on the bed, turns and looks towards The Orb.

"First, set the alarm clock on your phone.
        At least one hour before you leave for school."

Vinnie checks that he wrote that down correctly as it is a repeat from this morning, doing so his mind wanders.

> *At least I will get to play Twice Weekly before school if I do this.*

The Orb continues as it mistakes the glazed look across Vinnie's eyes and half-smile as a sign he is contemplating the benefits of this technique already.

"By setting the alarm YOU are taking control of YOUR day.
        YOU are going to give yourself time to get ready without having to rush.

This means you will be less likely to fall down the stairs and less likely to spill cereal into your lap.

        You will feel less stressed and get to school with time to spare."

The Orbs next instruction causes Vinnie to stop writing.

"Secondly, you will think of something you are grateful for that happened during the day.

        Write it in your notebook to add extra power to the words."

Vinnie casts a curious look at The Orb.

"I dunno about that bit. Sounds stupid. I will feel like a right div writing that down.... 'ooohhhh I am sooooo grateful'.......... I mean who does that??......"

These doubts were expected by The Orb, for it understands the concept of thoughts being so powerful as to actually alter the perspective of the world around them is quite something to grasp. For it goes against everything the boy has been taught.

The Orb pauses for a moment, as it contemplates how best to explain it to Vinnie.

Meanwhile, Vinnie is sat on the bed with a curious expression on his face as he watches the now silent Orb.

A few brief seconds pass with both Vinnie and The Orb sitting in silence.

Vinnie's curiosity gets the better of him, he leans forward so that he may try and poke at The Orb with his pen.

Just as he does so, The Orb speaks again causing Vinnie to jump slightly almost shoving the pen up his own nose.

"It will feel strange at first, Hero, that is sure.

Anything new usually does.

But remember, that feeling of resistance to this quite simple act of writing a sentence down is being caused by Brenda.

The Egolian inside of you feels threatened by it. That alone must show you how powerful it will be.

Trust me, Hero.

By thinking of and recognising something you are grateful for, even if your day appears to have been a disaster, emits an incredibly positive vibe, a positive vibration.
Remember our 'Law of Vibration'? It will pick up on this positivity and send more your way."

The Orb pauses to allow Vinnie time to write this all down.

The concentration causes Vinnie's tongue to poke out slightly at one corner of his mouth.

"Number Three.

Read the following sentence out loud to yourself every night:

'*When I wake up I will feel super energised and excited for the day ahead.*'

Imagine waking up and actually feeling what the words suggest."

Vinnie rolls his eyes at this but remains silent.

"Remember Hero,
try and make it the last thing in your mind before you go to sleep.

Your brain will remember this good feeling,
and that is what will feel upon waking."

Writing down the information in his notepad, Vinnie's tummy rumbles loudly. His mind starts wondering about what is for dinner that evening.

I hope it's not stew; I hate stew, it always has manky onions in it. Who even likes onions?!? Bleuuuggghhhh. It doesn't smell like stew....

Again, The Orbs voice brings him back into the room.

"Think about when you go to bed, on Christmas Eve or if you are going on holiday the next day.

You are excited and looking forward to what the new day will have to offer.

I bet you always wake up early and with a smile on your face those days!"

Vinnie smiles as he remembers last Christmas morning, it was the day he got the Edgebox.

The Orbs voice again penetrates his thoughts.

"Four.
When the alarm goes off.
You must wake up immediately.

DO NOT hit the snooze button."

Vinnie looks at The Orb, doubt once again etched across his face.

"That bit may be a bit tricky.
The bed is so cosy and warm."

The Orb fully understands the attraction of the duvet. It had taken advantage of its warm embrace whilst Vinnie was at school earlier and had enjoyed a nap for nearly 2 whole hours.

"I have a tip to make it easier to stick to.

As soon as the alarm goes off, start counting down from 5."

The Orb continues with its explanation.

"Counting will prevent Brenda from filling your mind with reasons to stay in the Comfort Zone.
For your brain cannot actually think of two things at once.
Whilst counting, throw back the duvet and stand up.
Have a good stretch of the hands to the ceiling if you fancy."

Vinnie's pen seems to be whizzing across the page as he is writing as fast as he can to keep up.

"By getting straight up you are sticking to a plan.

Albeit a simple plan of setting an alarm and getting up –
the 'Law of Vibration' will get positive vibes from this.

It will see you as a Hero who makes plans and sticks to them."

The Orb is now at the final tip.

"Five.

Make the bed.

Do this before you leave the room to have your morning poo..... ..."

Vinnie cannot help himself but interrupt The Orb.

"Hahaha, make my bed??
Really though,
what is the actual point of that!!"

He has never made his bed.

Sure, his mum does it sometimes, but that's what mums like to do, right?

"I mean, it's just a waste of my time Orby thingy.
I am only gonna get back into it
at night and mess it up again."

The Orb explains the significance of this action.

"By making your bed in the morning, you are already accomplishing a task.

This will give you a sense of achievement which will then impact the rest of the day.

The 'Law of Vibration' will offer more opportunities for achievements."

Vinnie stops writing and goes to rub out this last sentence.

"Nah, we can skip this one!"

The sound of a voice shouting from downstairs interrupts him.

"Dinnnnnnnnerrrrrrrrrrrrrrr!!!"

Vinnie immediately jumps up.

"Great. Hope its spag bol. I love that!"

He leaves the room and heading downstairs towards the smell of freshly cooked food.

Vinnie walks back into the room some 30 minutes later.

"Yep, Spagola it was!"

There is now a slight orange tinge around his lips and a similar orange mark is smudged along the back of his right hand.

"And my bad luck just got a whole lot worse."

He confides to The Orb.

"My mum is so annnnnnnnnoying.
Doesn't matter how many times
I asked her at dinner,
and it was loads.

She still refuses to buy me a new controller.
It's so flippen unfair. She has now told me if I keep on at her
she will make me wait till Christmas.

Christmas though!! That's aaaages away.

Couldn't even ask Dad, he was out again.
He is always out at the moment and mum is always mooooody."

Vinnie stares around the room, his breath quickening as he looks for
something to throw to vent the anger building inside of him.

The Egolian is smiling with glee, its excitement building ready for
Vinnie's total loss of control
and ultimately increasing
the chances of being stuck forever in the comfort zone.

But, instead of lashing out and causing a ruckus which would most
certainly have ended with his mum coming charging into the room and an
almighty row ensuing.

Vinnie did a curious thing.

He sat on his bed closed, his eyes and inhaled slowly through his nose.

Then exhaled slowly out through his mouth.

After a few breaths in and out his fists began to unclench.

Any thoughts of angry destruction dissolved.

Sniff the fart.......

.................."

Blow the burp.......

Brenda is now in total shock. It lets out a teeny tiny squeak as it feels itself shrink ever so slightly.

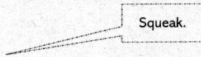

Squeak.

As Vinnie opens his eyes again, The Orb's glow is astonishingly bright.

"Hero, that was utterly amazing!! How do you feel?"

Vinnie reflects for a moment before answering The Orb.

"Well Orby, I feel alright.
Um, like my head is a bit more clear.
I did feel my tummy almost loosen a bit.
Do ya think I might need a runny poop?"

Vinnie remains in a state of calmness as The Orb responds.

"Oh, no Hero.

Not at all.

You have shown Brenda who is boss and the tummy feeling has nothing to do

with your bowels but everything to do with Brenda shrinking ever so slightly.

You are winning Hero; you are already winning!"

The Orb chuckles gently to itself as Vinnie smiles broadly at the winning comment.

"Hero, if you fully commit to the 'Power of Five' that I am teaching you, I can guarantee it will not only improve your whole morning, day and life.

It will also encourage your mum to buy you a new controller BEFORE your birthday."

Vinnie stares at The Orb, unsure as to whether this is a joke or not.

The Orb continues with his offer.

"It is true! Your birthday is in six weeks, correct?"

Vinnie nods slowly in agreement, still slightly suspicious at The Orbs declaration.

"So, for the next few weeks, you are unable to play on the Edgebox.
This means you can offer me a just over a month's commitment to master Brenda and change your mum's mind.

If by the end of that time nothing has improved I will be gone forever, and you will be able to wallow in the Comfort Zone."

The Comfort Zone doesn't seem such a bad place now that Vinnie realises it means he will not have to make his bed AND gets to play on the Edgebox.

But what if I get bored and find I am stuck forever...........
.........The Orb was right about the
fart sniffing and burp blowing........
What if it is right about this?

Vinnie ponders it for a moment.

Before standing up tall and declaring...

"Yeah, ok let's do this thing!"

If the Orb had a hand they would have shaken on it right then to seal the deal.

Later that night when drifting off to sleep, Vinnie did as he had promised.

"When I wake up I will feel
energised and excited for the day ahead..."

Well, well, **Reader of the Words...** What an **interesting** turn of **events!** I shall **not lie** to you. I **did not** like **school** much. *Way* too **noisy** and busy. Lots of *small humans.*

I **saw** some *really small ones* during that **assembly** thingy sticking a finger up their nose, **pulling out** a rather **unpleasant looking substance** and *popping it in their mouth.*

Is that the **usual snack** for a school child?? Seems an **odd** place to store **food.**

Anyways, do **you think** our Hero will *listen to* **the Orbs** instructions?

Hold on to your pants of the unders, **Reader,**

My rhyme is **bubbling up**.......

The school was LOUD and not much fun today,
Too much work, not enough play.
I would not go back there tomorrow,
Unless you have earmuffs I can borrow.

They have weird tests called SAT's.
I am most confused by that.
I saw all the children could sit easily,
Testing for that seems ever so silly.

Our Hero, he gets really mad,
When things don't go to plan or make him sad.
The Orb has offered him some things to do,
At bedtime and in the morning, before he heads to the loo.

Some simple tasks, nothing too tricky,
But will he do it? He is rather picky.
I guess with no other option to choose,
What does our Hero have to lose?

He will set an alarm for early morning,
I am sure the hour will set off some yawning.
A sentence to write, something grateful for,
And another to say, not much of a chore.

Morning alarm will ring loud, snooze he must not,
Straight out of bed: 5,4,3,2,1, like a shot.
His bed he must make, a task well done,
The good vibes created will ask for more fun.

I am not sure he believes they will work well,
Is The Orb joking? For he cannot tell.
But the risk he is willing to go ahead and take,
Especially if more compliant his mum it will make.

He wants his controller back, where it does belong,
Its missing presence feels ever so wrong.
Desperate to get it back so he can play,
But I bet the universe will send better things his way.

Look, look, Reader. His notebook lies there,
Showing the things, The Orb did just share.
Go have a look, I'm curious to see,
What thing did make our Hero happy.....?

The power of five

1. Set the alarm clock. At least one hour before you leave for school

2. Think of something that happened today that you are grateful for.

It does not have to be a big thing, anything which made you feel good.

Write it down. Makes it more powerful.

I am grateful

3. <u>Read</u> the following sentence <u>before going to bed.</u>

'<u>When I wake up I will feel energised and excited for the day ahead.</u>'

<u>Feel it,</u> like you do at special times like birthdays or Christmas.

Tomorrow gona be <u>fab!</u>

Part1p...

**The Power of Five is adapted from: Hal Elrod's 'The Miracle Morning'

4. When the morning alarm goes off, do not snooze it. Get up straight away!!

6.30

ALARM
OFF
OK?

BRINGGG!!

It may help to start counting down from 5. This stops Brenda trying to keep me in 'comfort zone' mode.

But it's warm in bed. Stay...

BLOCKED

5,
4,
3,
2,
1.

5. Make my bed. ~~before I go for a poo.~~

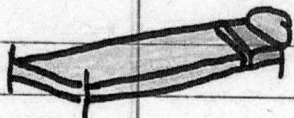

It will attract good vibes......

Good Vibe

Good Vibe

Good Vibe

Good Vibe

I am grateful that The Orb did not blind me with a flying sock this morning.

Tuesday.

Reader, **Reader**, welcome back. I *trust* you had a **pleasant** *rest.*

That **Will Smith** fellow, I checked him out on the net of inters and would you believe he has made over **48 movies.**

You can feel his self-belief and determination flow **strongly** through his words. What an **inspiration!**

Well, **our Hero** has agreed to the plan The Orb suggested.

He did indeed *think* of *something* he was **grateful for**; even though his day was most un of the pleasant.

It was rather lucky, don't you agree Reader, that the *dirty sock* did not *hurt his right eye.*

Miracles are found when **one looks closely**.

It is also **extraordinarily lucky** that it was only a **sock** and **not a dirty pair of pants** which pinged into **his eye.** I am not sure The Orb will *ever recover* from his own *flying laundry* situation; **our Hero** really should make sure **he** has *wiped* until the ***toilet paper is clear***. That *poor*, poor **Orb**.

Oh, my **Reader**, do *you see* what **happens** when *I chat with you?* My **mind** it does a **wander!**

I myself *heeded* The Orbs **advice** and *wracked my own brains* to **think** of something I am **grateful for** from the previous day's events. I came up with this.
"I am grateful that I did not go permanently deaf from my experience at the school."

I really am **grateful** too! My ears have only *just recovered!*
Thank *goodness* we do not need to **ever return** to that place again.

Huh?! **Reader** whatever *do you mean??*
Surely you are **doing** the *leg of the pulling*. We must return to that place **today?**

EVERY DAY you say? No, No, No, that will **never do**, I *cannot* go there **again** it is *too much to bear*.

*Reader, **Reader**. I know* you speak the truth, my fear of the school is just my Egolian Norman trying to keep me away from things and experiences which will **help me** on the road to **success.**

But even so, **Schools** give me the willies...... **Reader**, why *do you* laugh at me?

What did I say? I only said schools **give** me the **willies.** Well, *there you go again*. **Reader** tell me, *what is so funny?*

Oh, my day of days, I must **remember** not to use that word again, I thought it meant *scared*. **Dear me**, I fear I am **all of a blush**.

Ahem, anyways, back to the *subject of schools*. It **cannot** be true that we must go there *every day*.

What is that *you say*, **Reader?** A *week of ends* is a period of time away from the **school?** Oh **please**, *please* let us be on the verge of a **week of ends**.

So many **new things** to remember, my *brain is hurting*. It must be **Norman** for he cannot be **loving** all this *new learning* I am experiencing.

Now, where was I? Oh yes, I remember....

Our Hero did read the sentence out loud before bed last night, not too loud though for he did not want others in the house to hear him, but, read it he did before switching off his light.

There he is now; he sleeps so soundly again; it is nearly time for waking.

The alarm is set, about to go off. I will cover my ears for I do not like loud noises, they penetrate right through me. Get ready, Here it goes........

BRRRRRIIIIIIIINNNNGGGGGG!

It is 7:00 am and the phone alarm goes off an hour earlier than mum would normally try to wake him.

A skinny arm shoots out from under the duvet, grabs the phone and jabs at the button to silence it.

As the arm sneaks back under the covers a small voice can be heard whispering 5..,4...,3...., 2.. and as the voice says 1 Vinnie sits up.

Climbing out of the bed, he stretches his arms high above his head whilst simultaneously letting out a long yawn and a loud trumpet-like fart.

Lowering his arms, he goes to walk out of the room.

Vinnie suddenly remembers that he needs to make his bed. He pulls the duvet over the bed and pillows. He lifts the pillows out and places them on top of the duvet like he had seen his mum leave it. Once that is complete he shuffles out of the door towards the bathroom.

Vinnie does not spot The Orb watching from the top of the wardrobe. Its glow getting brighter as the boy makes the bed.

It begins to follow Vinnie out of the bedroom, stopping abruptly just outside the bathroom door as it remembers what is about to take place.

Returning to the bedroom The Orb hovers just above the freshly made bed happy to wait for Vinnie's return.

A good 15 minutes later he reappears, still yawning sleepily. The Orb greets him with cheerful tones.

"Good morning Hero! What a wonderous start to the day we have had."

Sitting on his freshly made bed, Vinnie rubs his eyes and mid-yawn turns to The Orb.

"I don't feel any different. You said I would feel good.
I just feel tired and wishing I was still in bed."

The Orbs cheery nature continues to shine through with words of encouragement to the sleepy boy.

"Hero, these first steps have given the day a taste of positive vibes.

More are sure to follow.

At first, it will just be a whisper of positivity; you may struggle to recognise it. But mark my words.

If you do the five simple tasks daily then the positivity will start to appear more loudly and become more noticeable."

The Orb pauses for a moment before continuing.

"Hero, you do know I am not a genie. Right?

You did not rub a lamp to get me here.

I do not promise the magic of fairy tales.

What I am offering you is much better than that,
a power to live your best life filled with all your hopes and dreams coming true."

A slightly bored-looking Vinnie glances nonchalantly around his room.

"Yaddda yadddda, yadddddda. Honestly Orb you do keep on. What am I supposed to do with this extra time anyway?"

The glowing Orb floats towards Vinnie as it speaks.

"Well, Hero.

Relax and get ready for school
and let's see what happens."

At these words Vinnie stands up, gives another stretch and pointing his bottom in The Orbs direction; lets out a long squeaky fart.

The Orb whizzes across to the other side of the room in an attempt to avoid the invisible cloud of stench now making its way towards it.

Vinnie heads out the door and walks down the stairs at a slower pace than the day before and as a result, does not slip.

He is also aware enough to catch sight of the floofy cat, hiding at the bottom step.

Its eyes are big as it is ready to pounce on an unsuspecting foot.

Deciding to take a leap at Vinnie as he reaches the final step, but Vinnie is too quick, he swings his foot just high enough for the floofy cat to miss.

The momentum of its attack continues to propel
the floofy cat through the air,
past where the boy's foot should have been
causing it to crash headfirst into the bannister.

Landing on the floor with a bump,
it shakes its head embarrassed.
Before darting ferociously through the hallway
and out of the cat flap
sporting an 'over it' look upon its floofy face.

Heading into the kitchen, Vinnie finds his mum sat at the table, holding onto a cup of lukewarm coffee as though it is a dear friend and staring blankly into her phone.

"Blimey Vin, You're up early!! Should I be worried??"

She exclaims, looking up at the kitchen wall clock certain it is going to tell her she is running super late.

He begins to mumble a reply at her.

"Morning mum, I'm just trying out a new ..."

His voice trailing off when he realises his mum is not listening to him. Her attention has returned to the phone screen.

Honestly, though. Grown-ups.
They moan about how much time us kids spend on a screen, yet they do it themselves, she is probably scrolling through Bookface ....yawwwwwn.

Vinnie opens the cupboard, and his frustration turns to delight as he discovers that his favourite cereal has returned.

Happily, he pours himself a generous helping into a bowl. As he is not rushing he is able to pour the right amount of milk into the bowl. Usually, there is a splash or two which do not make it and his mum moans at him to clean it up.

A small smile of satisfaction creeps across his face as he turns to see his mum's attention is momentarily on his milk pouring, her mouth opens slightly.

Haha! She thought I was gonna spill it!

Vinnie sits at the table, pretending not to notice the look on his mum's face or the fact that her eyebrows are raised so high in disbelief they might actually fall off.

Feeling content, Vinnie spoons the cereal into his mouth. A tiny dribble of milk starts to drip down his chin, but he stops it going any further with a well-aimed swipe of his pyjama top sleeve.

Finished and satisfied, he places his bowl on the side, and disappears out the door leaving his mum watching after him with curiosity.

Back in his bedroom, Vinnie dresses for school in no time.

He nips to the bathroom and brushes his teeth; managing to suck up a blob of toothpaste thus thwarting its attempt to jump from his mouth and all down his school sweatshirt.

Triumphantly returning to the bedroom, he plonks back down on the bed and turns to The Orb.

"Ready! And I still have 30minutes before I have to leave for school."

At this declaration, Vinnie grabs his phone and plonks down on the bed.

"I am going to play a game on my phone. If I can't play on my Edgebox, then this is the next best thing."

The Orb hovers close.

"Hero, do you think this is the best use of this newfound time?"

Vinnie dismisses The Orb.

"Shuuuuuush!"

The half an hour goes quickly.
A voice travels up the stairs and rouses Vinnie from his phone.

"....We are leaving in five minutes.
If you don't leave now you may as well walk with us......."

Mum getting ready to leave for school with his little brother, who is in year 3.

Do I want to walk with you?
Not bliddy likely!!!!

Vinnie thinks to himself, aghast at the suggestion, as a year 6 pupil walking to school with their mum AND irritating little brother is sooooo last year.

"No. I will walk by myself. Thanks......"

He quickly calls back; Grabbing his stuff and rushing out the door before she has a chance to catch him up.

He is off up the road and on his way to the school gates feeling unusually optimistic for the day ahead.

Outside the school is once again a chaotic combination of parents ushering small children across the road, whilst the lollipop lady holds back the traffic.

This particular lollipop lady is very chatty and loud. Her voice can often be heard keeping parents and children updated with the coming events.

"Don't forget chiiiillllllldreeeeen,

muuuufti day next week.

Dress as a book characterrrrr."

Announcements like this are usually followed by parents looking a little bit troubled as they remember that they are going to have to buy or worse still create a masterpiece by next Thursday.

Vinnie hurries past, without paying the lady in yellow too much attention. He will not do what he did last year though; borrowing his mums fake tan and going as an Oompa Loompa from Charlie and the Choc factory was brilliant at the time. Not so much a week later when he was still fairly orange and fed up with being called 'Satsuuuuma' by his mates.

The headteacher was not at the gate this time.

Vinnie has arrived early enough to go into the playground and hang about with his friends for a bit instead of being ushered straight into class.

He quickly locates his friends.

"Hi Vin.......
How comes you weren't on Edge
box again last night??
We had an awesome match."

"I was amazing. At one point I
managed to pass the ball all the way
down the pitch and boooom straight
over the goalie's head. Ya should've
seen it!!"

"Yeah Vin, ya
shoulda' seen
it.........."

The conversation makes Vinnie feel a bit left out and miserable.

This bed-making business had better make
mum get me that blasted controller..
It's so unfair ....

Vinnie's mates continued to chat about the football tournament game they all played the night before, giving each other stick about who was last in the league and arranging to have a rematch later.

Vinnies's mood is taking a turn for the worse.

The Egolian inside him perked up. Brenda had begun to worry that The Orb may have gotten through to the boy, but now its red fur was beginning to tingle in anticipation of some comfort zone chaos.

° o O ⟨ Hee Heeeeeee!! ⟩

The whistle was blown to signal the start of the school day, once again the children in years 3, 4, 5 and 6 lined up to be escorted in by their class Teaching Assistant.

The earlier years 1 and 2 are kept with their parents until time to go in and then greeted at the door. There is always at least one young child who has other ideas about how their day will go, and the parent has to chase them around the playground.

Vinnie's class were now at their seats, Mr Winterbottom arrives and begins taking the register. This time Vinnie is not chatting to his classmate, not because he cared about the register but because he is once again thinking about how unfair his mum is by not letting him have a new controller.

No contoller for you..

The Egolian inside him is thrilled.

If the boy is too busy looking at past events and wallowing about the unfairness of it all then he would not be focusing on the now. It would most definitely lead to a life in the Comfort Zone.

The first lesson of the day was English.

Not Vinnie's favourite subject.

Made worse today as it is leading up to an assessed write.

An assessed write is where the teachers and teaching assistant offer no help whatsoever, except for continually uttering phrases like:

'Stay focused',
                    'remember all we have taught you',

                                        'No, you cannot go to the toilet'.
and

          'Whoever threw that pencil across the room will have 3 strikes against their name.'

Today the class are to create a storyboard, this will be the basis of their written work tomorrow.

Vinnie used to be able to come up with stories but more recently has struggled to find one single decent idea, and today was no exception.

He is meant to create a short story based on a journey through someplace and a clue which guides the character through the story towards the end.

It just seems like such hard work to Vinnie as he sat there contemplating the actual point of the task at all.

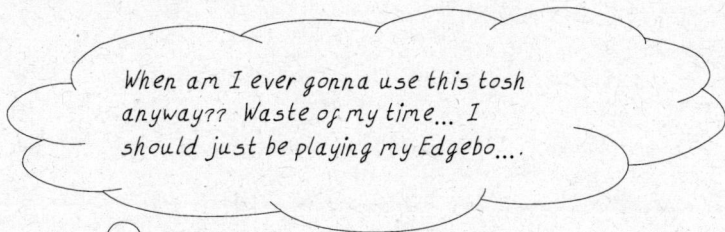

When am I ever gonna use this tosh anyway?? Waste of my time... I should just be playing my Edgebo....

His thoughts are interrupted by Helen, prodding his blank piece of paper.

"Well, Come on then. It's not going to write itself is it, Vinnie......"

Vinnie scowls inwardly at Helen's comment and now finds himself staring at the paper in front of him, unable to come up with a single idea. His hand gripping the pencil so hard his knuckles have turned white.

He closes his eyes ready to try 'sniffing the fart and blowing the burp' to see if that would help.

But Mr Winterbottom misunderstands and thinks that Vinnie is trying to get out of doing the work.

"Well, come on now Vinnie.
Less of the attitude.
If you don't get it done this lesson,
you shall be in tomorrow before school to do it."

This does not help at all; for now, Vinnie's mind is blanker than the piece of paper in front of him. It is blanker than Blanky McBlank face on a holiday in Blanksville.

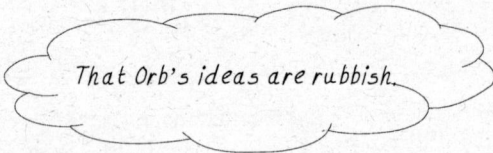

That Orb's ideas are rubbish.

It is the end of the lesson and Vinnie has managed to put nothing in his plan, he has a strike against his name AND he has to come in early tomorrow.

Vinnie is contemplating grabbing The Orb,
stuffing it under the duvet,
and punishing it with a full-on fart when he gets home.

Even a game of football at lunchtime did nothing to ease Vinnie's bad mood.

In fact, it added to it when he accidentally tackled his friend on the other team too hard. This resulted in being made to stand by the wall and get another strike against his name.
The end of the day arrives at last, and school is finally finished.
The frustration of yet another day etched on Vinnie's face.

The Egolian inside him is jumping up and down with glee at this most tiresomely awful day.

It is certain that annoying Orb will soon bog off and leave it and the boy to wallow in the comfort zone.

Walking slowly home, Vinnie kicks at stones whenever he comes across one lying in his path.

The Orb knows the day did not go well for its glow is duller than it has ever been, despite this its cheery optimism still shines through.

It understands that things take time, it is committed to creating the positivity needed to keep the Egolian at bay and the Hero on his rightful path.

The Orb just needs to convince the Hero.

Suddenly downstairs the front door slams and The Orb can hear heavy footsteps coming up the stairs, getting closer and closer.

They stop briefly on the landing.

"No, I don't want to play with you,
Do I look like a boring baby?"

The sentence is tinged with irritated venom.

"Oh, do what you like, go tell mum.
Mummy's boy.... Boo hoo hoo."

At this last sarcastic slur, the bedroom door bursts open.

The Orb is hovering above the bed, it moves quickly out of the way as Vinnie dumps his school bag on the floor and then launches himself across the bed, squishing up the pillows as he comes to a stop.

"Well, **thaaaaaaank yooooou** Orb."

He says turning to face The Orb, spittle flying from his mouth as he exaggerates the words.

"All I got from today was being made to leave my bed early, made my bed like some goody two shoes baby AND now I have to go into the school half an hour early tomorrow to do the work I did not do today."

Vinnie carries on with his rant before The Orb has a chance to speak.

"Mr WinterBUTThole even called my mum to ask that I come in early. AND she only said yes!!! What a flippen JOKE!"

Vinnie sits staring at his Edgebox, the new controller feeling further away than ever.

"And as if all that isn't bad enough, my annoying little brother thinks I am going to play with him.
Just because my controller is broken.
                Get.A.Life."

The Orb floats closer to Vinnie, its warm glow almost reaching Vinnie's feet which are planted firmly on the floor, Vinnie's arms are resting on his knees with his head held glumly in his hands.

He does not turn to face The Orb, instead continues looking wistfully at the unusable Edgebox.

...... I just want to play with my friends....
...... I JUST WANT TO PLAY WITH MY FRIENDS.....
......I JUST WANT TO PLAY WITH MY FRIENDS...

The Orb tries to be understood, its soft tones disturbing Vinnie's thoughts.

"Hero, I understand your frustration. I really do."

The calm tones from The Orbs voice do nothing to penetrate Vinnie's dark mood.

In fact, its very presence is adding to it.

"How do YOU know how I feel.
YOU are just a stupid ball of light.
Come to think of it, everything went wrong when
you showed up.
                    So Just BOG OFF!!!!"

Vinnie's tummy is feeling knotted once again, he is so frustrated at The Orb and his situation.

Brenda is fluffing up inside him.
The Egolian is spinning inside Vinnie.
the momentum of its spins creating an overpowering feeling of hopelessness in Vinnie.

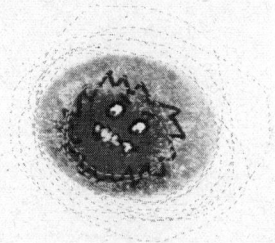

"Hero, I know you are feeling despondent about your current situation but do not let that cloud your thinking.

Remember if you are too focused on the feeling you will miss all the clues around you which will help you find a solution."

Once again The Orb attempts to get close to the disgruntled boy on the bed.

It floats around Vinnie, trying to get the warmth of its glow to penetrate Vinnie's thoughts and allow the words to sink in.

It is not having much luck.

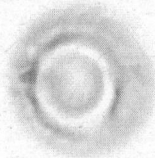

The Orb will not give up on Vinnie,
                    it cannot allow this Hero to be lost.

"The Egolian inside of you is growing stronger.

Before long you will be just another mediocre person plodding through life making it harder for yourself than it needs to be.

                                        Stuck forever in the Comfort zone."

Still getting no response from Vinnie The Orb continues.

"Hero, one way of dealing with a bad day is to replay it again in your mind, in your imagination."

This time Vinnie does respond, but not in the way The Orb had hoped.

"Brilliant Orb, yep just brilliant.
Going through this day again is sure to help me FEEL WAAAAAY BETTER. And anyway, my imagination wouldn't work in English today......"

But The Orb knows that this will indeed help Vinnie, so it continues with its attempt to sway the Hero.

"It will help Hero, close your eyes and imagine this day as you would have WANTED it to have turned out.

Try it.

You can just close your eyes and talk me through it.

I CAN help you."

The Orb quickly transforms into a set of headphones and secures itself firmly to Vinnie's ears before he can protest further.

After a short moment, Vinnie sighs heavily, he closes his eyes and begins.

"This morning was alright, not much I would change there. Except maybe my mum's phone would fall into her coffee at breakfast."

He giggles slightly as the image of his mum's face as her phone plops into a cup of lukewarm coffee plays out in his mind.

"I managed to get to school without having to walk with my divvy brother, so that was ok."

Vinnie starts to really relax and his imagination fires into life as he remembers more of the day's events.

"I saw my friends in the playground........
Hmmmmmmm, this time I have been able to play with them the night before and they are all well impressed that I managed to beat them and am now the leader of our football league."

As he speaks a smile spreads across Vinnie's face, he imagines them all excited and trying to get Vinnie to share his gaming secrets with them.

"Now I am in my English lesson...
Mr WinterBUTThole and Helen are certain I am going to be rubbish again, they give each other looks that they think I can't see. At the end of the lesson, Mr WinterBUTThole chooses my work to read to the rest of the class.

I have written a story so amazing.
Mr WinterBUTThole falls off his chair, as he does so he accidentally kicks Helen in the bottom.

I can see him on the floor with his legs in the air.
Helen is standing looking confused and rubbing her bottom!
The whole class is laughing.
Alfie is laughing so much he almost pees his pants! It is brilliant!"

Vinnie is enjoying the new and improved day very much.

The Egolian inside him not so much.

Vinnie continues to re-imagine his day, clearly enjoying the show in his head.

"I have an awesome game of football at lunchtime. I score three goals and am declared man of the match by all my friends.

Some of the kids in the lower years are cheering me too. No one gets hurt during the game and my friends are telling me I am just as awesome in real life football as I am on the Edgebox."

At this Vinnie raises a clenched fist above his head in silent jubilation. His re-imagined day is about to get a whole lot better!

"As I am walking home from school I find some money on the path. It's a five-pound note, just lying in the street. There is no one around who seems to have lost it."

"So, I pick it up and head to the sweet shop. I have
bought chocolate, sweets, and some fizzy pop.
Now I am lying on my bed with a full belly,
the fizzy pop makes me do the most enormous burp!
It is so loud the window shatters and explodes!
I am now about to play my friends on Twice Weekly."

At this last statement, Vinnie goes quiet and just lays there for a while,
allowing happy feelings to wash over him.

Meanwhile, The Orb returns to its normal shape and hovers just by the bed,
waiting.

After a short while, Vinnie sits up.
He turns to The Orb.

"Ya know what Orbster.
That did make me feel better.
Helen's face as she got kicked in the bottom,
Alfie peeing his pants, and THAT burp!"

However, Vinnie's smile turns to a frown once again as the re-imagined day
fades away and a thought enters his head.

"That 'new' day was fun and all but,
I still don't have my controller
and I still have nothing to do."

The Orb hovers over Vinnie's notebook on the side.

"Hero, you have such positive vibrations in you right now.

Choose to keep them.

Remember positive vibes attract positive things. Write down the technique we just did so that you don't forget."

The room is silent for a moment as Vinnie writes the re-imagining technique in his book.

Vinnie's attention has returned to his re-imagined day as he remembers the teaching assistant getting a kick in the butt by the teacher falling from his chair.
This time though, something else is playing on his mind.

"One thing though Orbster, in my new imagined day some things happened like the teacher falling off his chair.
                    and Alfie nearly peeing his pants.

It did cheer me up because it was kind of funny, but because it was like bad stuff happening to others, will it still be able to bring positive stuff to me?"

The Orb is extremely impressed by this question.

"Well, Hero, that is a clever question. I am glad you asked."

The Orb is full of fresh hope that this Hero really does have what it takes to master the Egolian within him.

"As long as the new imaginations are like that of a funny movie where we know that the people don't really get hurt then it is ok.

If your new imaginations are on more of an angry and violent note then it will not produce those good vibes we need and will actually create the opposite effect."

Satisfied with that explanation, Vinnie picks up the notebook to jot down some further notes.

As he does so The Orb continues.

"After you have finished writing I suggest a good use of your evening is watching a movie.

Soul Surfer is an excellent choice.

You will see what real determination looks like.

Are you ok with sharks?"

Vinnie smiles, as he does indeed like sharks.

"Sharks eh? Well, I will need to ask my mum, she may be wanting to watch one of her boring shows..."

Vinnie returns to his notebook and as he finishes off his writing he turns to The Orb, a desperate tone in his voice.

"But what about tomorrow. How am I *really* going to make it better than today??"

The Orb moves close to Vinnie so he may feel the comfort of its warm glow as it offers some final words of encouragement.

"Hero, you have already begun to make tomorrow a whole lot better than today.

Now, enjoy the movie.

Remember to write down what you are grateful for.

Read the sentence before bed.

Tomorrow is another day.

You'll see......."

Later that evening.......

"Hmmm, when I wake up tomorrow I will feel energised and excited for the day ahead."

Reader, I *must confess*. That school business was **not so bad** for me today.

It is definitely **less scary** than the day before. I might actually *get used* to all the noise!

I get a sense **The Orb** may be *getting through* to our Hero, do you?

Amazing **things** are on the way **HOORAH!!** I can feel it. I can feel it in my rhyme....

Our Hero's morning was much improved,
He made his bed before he pooed.
The Orb was wise and did not follow,
It remembered the stench was hard to swallow.

Safely downstairs our Hero moved,
The cats failed attack left it quite bemused.
Into the kitchen, our Hero strode,
His sleepy mum was on her phone.

He smiled when he saw her stare,
wondering why he was there.
The hour was early, she was surprised,
He is normally still sleepy-eyed.

His smile continued when he did find,
The cereal was his favourite kind.
No milk was spilt, or pyjamas wet,
This morning was his best yet!

The day did take a turn for the worst,
Brenda's negativity did burst.
It made him think in fits of despair,
"Why me? It's just not FAIR!!"

It did not improve later at all,
At lunchtime, he did lose his cool.
The day left him feeling down,
His face carried an angry frown.

The Orb it made our Hero smile,
he closed his eyes and lay there awhile,
reimagining his day, it was quite fun,
The poor assistant got kicked in the bum.

The Orb has more wisdom to share tomorrow,
To stop our Hero feeling such sorrow.
He needs to quickly learn that in his mind,
The _power_ to change things he _will_ find.

Reader, look at the notebook there,
The reimagining technique it will share.
We too will be able to reinvent our day,
To make sure OUR positive vibes do stay!

Make a BAD day better

1. Lie down and close your eyes.

2. Can listen to the music if you want but don't have to.

3. Help relax yourself by:

Sniffing the fart
Blowing the burp

4. <u>Start to replay the day in your head.</u> Picture it as you would have preferred it.

Remember:
It can be as random as you like.

Think of it as a <u>funny</u> <u>slapstick movie</u> where no one really gets hurt.

ha ha ha

I am grateful my favourite
cereal was in the cupboard. It
was yummy!

Movie
to
Watch

Wednesday.

'Start where you are. Use what you have. Do what you can.'

Arthur Ashe

Well **Reader** what an interesting evening our **Hero** had. He did indeed watch 'Soul Surfer', and *do you know* who else **watched** it too?

His mum.

Not his dad though, he went out, he did not seem to be very happy.

But his mum did.

She was **so intrigued** about the request to watch a **movie** she said they should watch it after his little brother had gone to bed. It even **overran** our **Hero's** bedtime, but mum let him stay up until the end of the movie.

I will tell you a secret.

His **mum** *enjoyed* the movie. she also enjoyed sitting with Vinnie on the sofa. It has *been a while* since they have done that together as our **Hero** is often on the Edgebox.

Mum also made a *rather strange* **foodstuff**.

It **started** as *hard lumps* and it was in a pan on the **cooker thingy**.

It went pop. pop. poppity. pop. pop for what felt like **aaaaaages**

and gave off a wonderful **aroma** as it did.

When the lid came off the **pan** it had **transformed** into these fluffy looking balls!!

Most extraordinary **Reader**. *most extraordinary!*

I had a *sneaky peek* at the **movie** too and that **Bethany**.

Wow! Such determination.

Hmmm, I *wonder* if our Hero will copy some of that **die-hard desire** to succeed in his English lesson today.

I *noticed* that **our Hero** also completed the tasks set by **The Orb**, even though the *hour was later* due to the **movie**.

A **grateful thought** was *written down* and **a sentence** *said aloud*. Two nights in a **row** that must be *giving off* some **positivity.**

The **Hero's** imagination got a ***jump start*** yesterday with The Orbs *reimagining technique* - most enjoyable to **watch!**

I will *let you in* on another **secret** Reader. I also had a little go of the **reimagining technique**. Do you want to *know how it went?*

Oh goody, I was *hoping you would!*

Well, I imagined **all** the **children** in *the school* had lost their **voices** for the whole day! **It** was marvellous, the children though were most flummoxed.

They were *opening and closing* their mouths looking like a shoal of confused fish. The teachers were *so shocked* they **closed** the **school** in case it was contagious, and everyone went home.

The week of ends had arrived **early**....
Hooooraaaahhhhh the **children** mouthed, *silently* hi-fiving each other as they walked out the **school** gates.
Only to have their **voices** return the moment they got **home**.
Their **voices** came back louder than ever, and all the **parents** had to go out and buy **big woolly earmuffs**.
Such **fun!**
Oooh, and I took a peek at that Steven Spielberg chap *on the* net of inters.
He never let his **dream** fade. He could *easily* have let his own Egolian **trap** him in the comfort zone. He **suffered** from **bullying**, he was **rejected** by his dream university and *depressed* about his **future**. But his determination to **succeed** was so

strong he **defeated** all those obstacles and became a **huge** success. He has

produced some **awesome** movies.

That **Jurassic Park** looks aaaaaamazing.

I thought dinosaurs had died out *millions of years ago*, yet

Spielberg managed to **find** some *of them* and *get them* to **do** all sorts of

wonderful acting.

Reader? Reader, **why** *do you* laugh at me?

You *say* the Dinosaurs are **not** real??

I am most con of the fused. They looked remarkably real to **me**.

Why I *nearly* did poop my metaphorical pants when a dinosaur came

lurching out of the screen!!

Gosh, here we are **again** chatting away.

Let's **not forget** that our Hero must go into school a little earlier today to do the *task* he couldn't complete **yesterday**.

I wonder how that will go.

School is not his favourite thing at the moment.

It *must be* soon for one of those week of ends you told me about.

Huh?! *Three* more *days* you say, **Reader**, *three more until the week of ends??*

Oh, my goodness gracious how will we surrrrrrrrrrrvivvvvvvvvvve .... Oh, woe is meeeeeeeeeee!

Ahem, yes sorry **Reader** you are right.

I must **pull** *myself together.*

I believe my *Egolian Norman* is turning me into a queen of the drama.

I must stay focused on our **Hero.**

Let us **go** into his **room** and *see how he is.*

Vinnie is lying sprawled across the bed the duvet is half on him and a half on the floor. His face squished into the pillow and a small river of drool is dribbling from his half-open mouth.

He mutters to himself as his eyes dart back and forth under his eyelids.

His phone is by the bed, this time primed to go off *even* earlier than yesterday so that he doesn't get into further trouble with his mum and Mr Winterbottom.

Suddenly.

BRRRRRIIIIIIINNNGGGGGGG!

"Gaaaaaaahhhhhhmmmphhh!!!!!"

Vinnie shouts as the sudden noisy intrusion causes him to momentarily lift his head off the pillow and then slam it back down again face-first into the drool.

He reaches out for the phone and turns it off with a whack.

Continuing to lay there for a moment, beginning to drift gently back into his slumber. He suddenly remembers his task for the day, and he gets sleepily up.

Yawning as he makes his bed Vinnie hauls the crumpled duvet off the floor and lobs it on the bed. Moving it around so it sits on the bed with the pillows on top. Not as neat as yesterday, but at least it is done.

Vinnie mooches out of the room to begin his morning routine. Shuffling to the loo as usual. (His poop schedule runs more efficiently than a bus timetable.)

A short while later, as Vinnie is leaving the loo and heading for the stairs the floofy cat spots his approach. After a pause it decides to leg it along the hallway without attempting to assassinate Vinnie's toes.

Mum is at her usual spot this time of the morning, in the kitchen with her coffee.
When she sees Vinnie enter the room, she puts down her phone and turns her attention to him.

"Blimey! You're up early again Vin!
I really enjoyed that movie last night,
who did you say recommended it?"

She asks standing up to playfully ruffle his untidy hair.

"Oh erm, just a friend at school. I liked it too. I don't think I would have ever got back into the water after having my arm bitten off."

Vinnie replies quickly, not wanting her to ask any further questions about what friend.
He walks towards the cereal cupboard.

As he does he can hear is mum behind him making a funny sound.

"derr den, derr den, da de da de da de da de derrrrrr"

He looks around just as she comes up behind him grabbing his arm and pretending to chew it off.

"Muuuuuuuuuuum!"

Vinnie exclaims giggling and wriggling.
She releases him ruffling his hair again and smiling at him as she does.

"Vin, I have been thinking........
about this Edgebox controller situation."

As she mentions the Edgebox controller Vinnie stops rummaging for a bowl and turns his attention to her.

"Well, I noticed that you made your bed yesterday and made an extra effort to get to school on time. And I know that Mr Winterbottom is not your favourite of teachers..."

She takes a sip of the now lukewarm coffee as Vinnie watches and waits with anticipation for her to continue.

"......... So, my thinking is.
if you can continue to show me
you are being more mature both at home and at school......"

At the word, 'mature', Vinnie's mind begins to wander.

Blimey oh Riley, Grownup's love using that word it's mental, why's it so important be to be '**mature**', I have seen cheese that's described as mature.

Does she want me to be a piece of cheese?

Luckily for Vinnie, his mum doesn't notice the distant look in his eyes while he ponders the cheese/mature phenomenon, and she carries on chatting.

"..... then we don't *have* to wait
until your birthday for a new controller."

Vinnie's attention suddenly pings back to his mum like a snapped elastic band.

Can it be that The Orb is actually right?

"Mum?! Do you mean it??"

The shock at this turn of events is evident on Vinnie's face as he stands there momentarily stunned, his mouth open wide like a whale shark.

Snapping out of his daze, Vinnie turns to his mum a broad smile stretching across his face.

"When do you think I will get a new one? Tonight??"

His mum responds laughing gently, smiling at her son's lit up face.

"Oh Vin, steady on!
Why don't we say..........,
if you can do an amazing job for Mr Winterbottom
today and continue to make your bed
showing me how mature you are.............
Then ...., I will buy you one next weekend."

Vinnie launches himself across the kitchen and hugs his mum.

"Best news ever!
Thanks, Mum!"

Vinnie cannot believe this turn of events, he is the happiest he has felt in ages, he feels like there is nothing that can bring him down!

"And another thing Vin. It would be great
if you could start being nicer to your brother too."

Nothing can bring him down.

Except maybe that.

Vinnie stops hugging his mum, stands away from her.

"Erm, no you're alright thanks."

As he responds he rolls his eyes so far back in his head he can nearly see his brain

Mum lets out a sigh at this retort, and taking a last mouthful of coffee, she places the cup on the sink and walks out of the room.

Leaving behind a super happy Vinnie, who is now humming as he makes his breakfast.

Meanwhile, back in Vinnie's bedroom, The Orb is also humming to itself as it looks around the room.

A bed is made, a Hero is up, poop has been had, a morning going very well indeed.
Its glow is bright. It can feel the positive vibes in the air.
The Orb is so caught up in the happy vibes it fails to notice a presence has entered the room.

A very floofy presence.
With eyes as big as saucers.

It spots The Orb twirling and humming a few centimetres off the top of Vinnie's bed.

It crouches low on the floor,
as flat as it can be,
and shimmies across the carpet.

The Orb, still floating and humming, fails to notice as the floofy cat moves closer to the bed.

It's attention is on the sun rising through a gap in the curtains.

The sky is tinged with pink, and the day is full of opportunities.

Having now reached the side of the bed the floofy cat pulls back ready to pounce, it's bottom wiggling as it primes its back legs ready for take-off.

At that very moment, a full and content Vinnie walks into the room his sudden presence startles the floofy assassin in its tracks.

YOWWWWLLLLLLLLLLL!!

Scarpering through Vinnie's legs zooming out of the door its claws catching on the carpet as it whizzes off down the stairs.

The Orb shoots straight up into the air as though a firework has just gone off up its bottom as the noise of the frightened cat startles it.

The force of the upward lift causes The Orb to hit the ceiling and splat against it. An amused Vinnie looks up at The Orb.

"Ha ha ha, Orbster
    you look like a fried egg on the ceiling..."

Vinnie continues to chuckle to himself as he finds his school clothes and dresses for the day ahead.

"... fried egg... ha ha ha
hmmmmmm,
now, where did I leave my trousers?"

A disgruntled Orb peels itself off the ceiling, its glow a slight embarrassed pink almost the same as the sunrise sky.

"Well, that was an eventful start to the morning Hero.
I best watch out for that four-legged felon in future."

Vinnie is now clutching a pair of already worn socks.
He sniffs them to check their cleanliness, pulls back slightly at the whiff.
Before deciding that actually, they are not too smelly and can last another day.

"Orby, it does make me question though,
who else will be able to see you?
I thought it was just me........."

Asks Vinnie, now nearly fully dressed and pulling on the crusty socks.

Floating back in its normal shape, The Orb settles next to Vinnie.

"An interesting question Hero.

It was indeed a wise decision of yours
not to allow me to accompany you to school."

Vinnie groans at the mere mention of the word school.

"Schooooool......
Now I have to make sure I can wow
Mr Winterbutthole even more since mum has said if I act
'Matuuuure' I will get a new Edgebox controller by next weekend."

The Orb lifts slightly, it hovers level with Vinnie's face.

It's joy at this new development evident in its dazzling glow.

"Next weekend?

That is good news Hero!

I told you the good vibes you gave out would send more your way, didn't I?!

Didn't I?!!"

The Orb almost sings the words, it is incredibly happy to have been proved right so quickly.

Vinnie however, clutches his tummy and his shoulders visibly deflate as he considers his situation.

"But how am I going to think of a story for
Mr WinterBUTThole when my brain either gets all blank or it fills with
all sorts of stuff nothing of which is ever any use to me and to top it
off my tummy makes me feel sick?"

The Orbs soothing voice offers some words of encouragement.

"Well, Hero.
Just remember that the physical feelings you experience are from the Egolian
inside you.

It does not want you to succeed.

It wants you to stay exactly as you are.

You must master it.

By doing so its effect on you physically will diminish.

It won't go away entirely but you will look forward to those slight feelings as
they will show you that you are on the path to greatness."

The words bounce around the room, and Vinnie's brain, as he sits in silence
for a moment pondering them.

The Orb is about to enlighten Vinnie with more wisdom when Vinnie stands
up and lets out a long puff of air.

"Well, Orby McOrbster, you have been right so far with regards to the Edgebox controller coming early. But how am I to master Brenda? If it was outside of me I would probably whack it with something until it did as it was told."

At this Vinnie grabs a discarded badminton racquet and whacks a pair of jogging bottoms on the floor until they are suitably mastered.

The Orb interjects this act of remarkable bravery against the jogging bottoms with yet more wisdom.

"Hero, you are already bestowed with the greatest weapon known to man. With it, you can master, conquer, and succeed at anything your heart desires."

Vinnie drops the racquet and turns his attention back to The Orb.

"Oooooooh....."

The Orb floats close to the boy's face and whispers in a dramatic echoey fashion.

"It is your mind........ and your will."

Vinnie blinks a couple of times, a little miffed it's not some sort of superweapon with blasters and a fart rocket.

"Huh?!"

The Orb continues.

"First, you must silence the chatter which fills your mind."

Vinnie looks blankly at The Orb his mind now full of images of fart rockets and blasters. One of his eyes doing a slight jitter and the corners of his mouth turning up slightly as he imagines blasting his brother full-on in the face with a 'wet and windy' one.

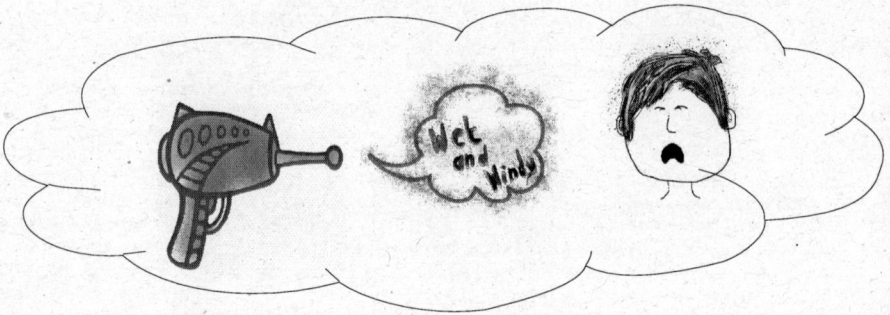

The Orb carries on regardless.

"The chatter in your mind is sometimes referred to as the 'Monkey Mind'. ....."

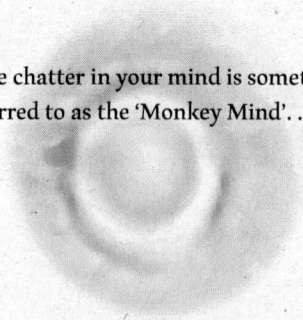

Vinnie's attention is back in the room at this recent revelation.

A worried look crosses his face as he ponders what The Orb has just divulged.

I have a monkey in my mind.
A Brenda in my belly and a monkey in my mind.
What am I? A blinkin zoo??

The Orb continues.

".....A person's brain is often filled with different thoughts, fleeting thoughts. It can often sound like this:

'Where did I leave that sock? Haha the cat is so funny. I really don't like school. I wonder what's for dinner. Is it nearly Christmas? What times lunch? Wish I hadn't shouted at Barry last week. What times lunch? Where is my pen? Do I need a poo? Should I go now in case......?'

The thoughts themselves differ from person to person but the chatter can be much the same..........."

The Orb is interrupted by Vinnie.

"Is it nearly Christmas?"

The Orb is already beginning to regret the examples it gave.

"Er, no Hero. I think you are missing the point somewhat....."

The Orb tries to interrupt so that it can continue its explanation, but Vinnie continues thinking out loud to himself.

"I don't need a poo I already had one.
I wonder what is for dinner.
School really is the worst..."

Suddenly and without warning, The Orb both silences Vinnie and freezes him in an instant. As before Vinnie is now a human statue sat on his bed. This time however only his eyes are working.

"Blink twice if you are ready to listen."

Vinnie, of course, blinks twice immediately and The Orb at once relinquishes its hold over the boy.

Not entirely though, just his head.

Vinnie is now able to move his head around, blink and speak.

Strangely though, Vinnie's bottom also appears to have regained its functions as it lets out a rather strangled sounding fart.

It catches Vinnie by surprise, and he lets out a slightly strangled giggle to match the fart.

"Phneehee-gwaaa-hee!"

The Orb decides to ignore the ill-timed butt squeak and continues.

"Hero, to tame the Monkey mind, we can do a remarkably simple exercise which requires nothing other than your breath and the ability to count to ten.

You can count to ten right?"

Vinnie rolls his eyes at The Orb's sarcastic line of questioning as The Orb transforms once again into a pair of headphones and secures itself snuggly on Vinnie's head.

Within seconds, the rest of Vinnie unfreezes, his body relaxes, his eyes close and he places his hand's palm down on his knees.

Meanwhile, the floofy cat has snuck into the room.

It struts in like it owns the place,
tail aloft, eyes darting softly around the room looking for something to pounce upon.

Suddenly it stops as its eyes come to rest upon The Orb currently fixed to Vinnie's head.

The floofy cat's eyes become wide like saucers and it stealthily crosses the room.

Only stopping when its nose accidentally comes to rest on a dirty pair of Vinnie's underpants abandoned in the middle of the room.

The cat moves expertly around the offending pair of pants.
Never once removing its gaze off the shining Orb.

It gently jumps on the table next to the bed, taking great care not to make a sound.

Vinnie and The Orb are totally engrossed in their activity and do not feel the slight dip in the duvet as the floofy cat makes its way on to the bed.

It shimmies over to Vinnie and The Orb.

Crouching down its back legs tensing, getting ready.

Until suddenly.

SSSSSPPPRONGGGGG!

The floofy cat launches itself straight at Vinnie's head just as The Orb has finished.

It spots the floofy cat mid-air and whizzes out of the way. Saving itself from the cat's clutches.

This lightning-quick move however, has done nothing to help Vinnie.

"AAAArrrrrrggggggggghhhhhhhhhhh!"

Vinnie lets out a shriek as the floofy cat lands upon his head, its claws digging into his scalp.
Instinctively Vinnies stands up and tries to shake the floofy cat from his head.

"AAAArrrrrrggggggggghhhhhhhhhh!"

This forces the cat to dig its claws in deeper still.

"AAAArrrrrrgggggggghhhhhhhhhh!"

A voice suddenly appears at the doorway.

"Blimey Vin...What is going on in here??"

The noise from the floofy cat's attack has woken Ben up and he has hurried in to see what the commotion was about.

He stands watching in amusement as Vinnie spins around on the spot wearing an angry cat hat.

Vinnie dips his head downwards and the gravitational pull helps him to dislodge the floofy cat which then whizzes through Ben's legs and disappears down the stairs.

"Owwwwwwwwwch!"

Vinnie exclaims as he sits on the bed rubbing his head and fighting the urge to cry.

"Vin, why did you put the cat on your head?"

Ben asks genuinely confused about the scene he just witnessed.

Vinnie stops rubbing his head and looks at his little brother as if he had just pulled him out of his own nose.

A mixture of disgust and disbelief.

"Oh, my Gawd. You're such a div.
Why would I put the blimmin cat on my head??"

Ben shrugs his shoulders and sits down on the bed next to Vinnie.

"The stupid thing went mental and jumped on my head.
All I was doing was sitting still on my bed,
with my eyes closed.
            Then whamma banga bing-bong,
                    the mental cat lands on my head."

Vinnie rubs his head again as he finishes explaining the chaos which had just occurred.

"But Vin, why were you sat up on the bed with your eyes closed?"

Ben has never seen his brother sit still for any reason before, even at the cinema Vinnie squirms and wriggles.

"I was listn....."

Vinnie begins to tell Ben the truth but stops suddenly remembering who he is talking to.

He does not want his irritating little brother to know what weirdness is going on.

"Erm, I was letting off a big gusty stinky fart!
that smelt of last night's spag bol.
A big gusty meaty fart,
that you are now sitting right in the middle of!"

At this, Vinnie wafts his hands into Ben's face as if he was scooping up the stench and poof it at him.

"Ewwwwwwww. You are so disgusting.
I'm gonna tell muuuuuum."

Ben jumps up immediately heading for the door, covering his mouth and nose with one hand.

As he heads for the door his eye catches a weird light coming from the top of Vinnie's wardrobe.

"What is that??"

Ben starts to head back into the room, but Vinnie jumps up and shoves him out the door.

"GO AWAAAYYYYY. Nosey little vegturd..."

Vinnie shouts as he slams his door in Ben's face.

"muuuuuuuummmmmm........"

The sound of Ben's voice trails off as he disappears downstairs to find mum. Vinnie turns his attention to The Orb who has now reappeared from the top of the wardrobe.

"Well, Hero, it seems the universe has little control over that furry feline...."

Vinnie rubs his head, wincing slightly as his hand brushes over a tiny puncture wound in his scalp from the outrageously sharp kitty claws.

"Ya think so Orb?!!!!"

Vinnie's response is dripping in a cocktail of sadness and sarcasm.
It is nearly time for school and Vinnie is starting to feel a knot in his tummy as he remembers that he has to come up with a story for Mr Winterbottom.

Brenda is churning up the feelings of doubt.

Vinnie starts to rummage for his school bag while The Orb hovers nearby.

"Hero, **start where you are**."

Vinnie looks up at The Orb puzzled.

"And what exactly is that supposed to mean?"

The Orb floats across the room towards Vinnie.

"Sit down, Hero. Just for a moment and I will explain.

Grab your notebook and jot this down.

I promise it WILL help."

Sighing heavily, Vinnie checks the time on his phone.

He has 10 minutes before he needs to leave so he shrugs and plonks his bottom on the bed.

With the pad in hand, he turns his attention back to The Orb.

"I call this – THE POWER OF NOW.

There are three parts to it.

The original phrase was coined by a man with extraordinary character and determination.

Start where you are.. means don't dwell on stuff that has already happened.

Write this down."

The Orb continues as Vinnie details it in his note pad.

"Everything that happened up until this moment is not important.

You cannot change past events.

But **you can control** how they affect **you**.
In this **present** time."

The Orb pauses briefly so Vinnie can catch up.

"So, Hero, start where you are, start afresh.
Begin again. Be reborn. Rise agai......"

Vinnie pauses writing for a moment as his attention is drawn both to The Orb currently in a full-on dramatic pep talk, and the disappearing time left before he has to leave for school.

"Alright, Orbster ....

I've not got all day......"

The Orb pauses...

"Yes, yes of course!"

.......and carries on....

"Use what you have."

Vinnie returns to his writing, keeping one eye on the time.

Being late is not an option this morning.

"Hero, you have an amazing brain!

You thought your imagination was gone.

Yet, it sprang back into life yesterday with the reimagining technique.

YOU created those images in your head.

YOU have the power to create."

As The Orb speaks, Vinnie's mind does indeed spring into life, recapping on the alternative day he imagined.

A small smile appears on Vinnie's face as his brain fills with the images.

"**Do what you can**."

Continues The Orb.

"You are in control, Hero.

Do not settle for the bare minimum.

Put in the effort and you **will be** rewarded."

Vinnie finishes writing and looks up at The Orb.
His face still showing obvious signs of anxiety.

The Egolian in him feeling fairly confident that every word The Orb just said whizzed through one of Vinnie's ears, bypassed the 'memory' section of the boy's brains and whizzed right out the other ear.

Nothing to see here.

"......and one more thing Hero.

Before you start to write at school today take a few moments to calm the 'monkey' in your mind.

This will make room for and allow the creativity to flow.

If you are not able to close your eyes just focus on something near you which will not move, like your pencil on the desk".

With that, Vinnie pauses for a moment to consider what The Orb has just told him.

As he does so, a small smile crosses his lips.

There is a tiny twinge of confidence bubbling under the surface, a small river of self-belief begins to flow.

The Egolian within him remembers the boy silenced it before with a sniff of a fart and a blow of a burp.

It prickles with fear.

Vinnie stands up, gathers up the rest of his things for school and heads off.

The Orb watches Vinnie from the window as he wanders off up the street towards school.

The Orb also decides that it will hide on top of the wardrobe for the rest of the day just in case the floofy cat comes back for another go.

Oh Reader, another **day,** *another* task for our **Hero** to complete.

This **life** business is an *endless* **stream** of tasks and **jobs**.

It does **not** seem to be **much** of the **'fun'**.

My **mood** feels *slightly* **faded** for I **do not** think The **Orb** can **save** this

Hero from the *comfort zone*.

Do you think **Norman** is filling **me** with **negativity?**

For my **energy** is *barely* there and **I** feel **like** saying:

'What's the **point**, let's just **give up'**.

Yes, yes **Reader** you are right it is **time** for a rhyme.

I am so **glad** you are following this **Hero's** Journey with **me**, or I

should be *very* **lost** indeed.

Yes, yes, a **rhyme** always **cheers** me up.........

Oooh, oooh, ahh, ahhhhh,
Ooooo, ohh, ah, ahhhhh.
Who'd of guessed we would find,
A monkey in our Hero's mind!

Its noisy chatter interferes,
The Egolian inside him cheers.
Off to school, our Hero goes,
Will he succeed? I just don't know!

To allow his imagination to flow,
The chatter in his head must go.
A count to ten, and then repeat,
His breath becomes slow and deep.

Hands are spread with palms face down,
Feet are firmly on the ground.
A back so straight it makes him tall,
Our Hero may be alright, after all.

Once again I see it there,
The notebook with great things to share.
Reader, go peek and you will find,
You can train the monkey in your mind!

You've had a look? Why you're no fool!
Come now, let's get off to school.
We can observe the writing test,
I really hope he tries his best.

The Power of NOW!

Start where I am.

Can't change past, only how it affects me

obsession

Anger

Acceptance

Positive

Sad

Calm

MY CHOICE

happy

fury

forward thinking

Without Power of Now.   With Power of Now.

Use what I have.

Focus on what I have, not what I don't have —

ME

- Positive thinking
- Sniff fart/blow burp awesome friends
- Mad football skills
- Imagination
  ability to fart for quite a long time

Do what I can.

Try super hard at all things and they will reward me!

Silence Monkey

Practice reading

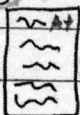

~At

revise at home

Make bed daily

help at home

breathe away anger

MAN o MATCH

Team player

Good sportsmanship

Practice Skills

Wednesday continues.

London Times Newspaper

BOY MORE CLEVER THAN POLICE!

A youngeth boyeth of twelveth doth manageth to cathcheth the Ripper of Old London Town.

The Ripper doth evadeth policeth for manyeth a montheth.

Policeth haveth nothing to sayeth about the mattereth.

Rumours are aboundeth that a keyeth of the magic sorteth is to thanketh.

The youngeth boyeth has denyeth any useth of a keyeth of magic.

When questionedeth, the boyeth states.

"I am just more clever than the police."

The juryeth is outeth on thateth oneth.

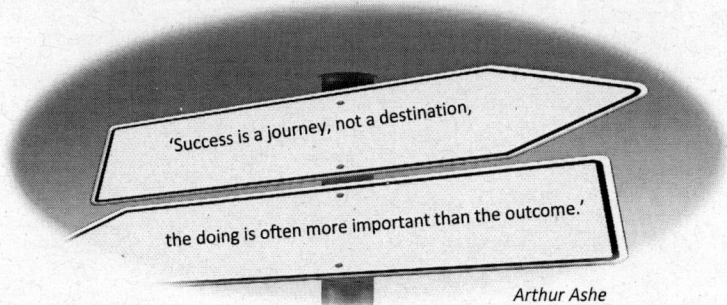

'Success is a journey, not a destination,

the doing is often more important than the outcome.'

Arthur Ashe

There he *goes* **Reader**, not as fast as he was heading into *school* on Tuesday.

Our Hero's **task weighing** heavy on his *shoulders*. See **reader**, see how he walks, **head down**, eyes on the *floor*, shoulders hunched?

That is **not** the **stance** of a confident Hero, most *certainly* **not**.

He must succeed or he will **lose** this **opportunity** to make his **mum** *proud* and turn this game controller situation around.

The **magnitude** of our Hero's task has made **my** own Egolian **Norman** twist in my **tummy**. I feel a *tad queasy*.

I fear our **Hero's** head is **full** of monkey *chatter* of the most **discouraging** kind – I can almost hear it **now** –

'you *can't write a story*.'

'you are no good.'

'**give** up now, **give** up now you smelly little **boy**'.

Ok, so *maybe* **not** the smelly little **boy** bit!!

But I bet the monkey chatter is **whirling** around his *head*.

Ya know what though **Reader**, that Arthur Ashe chap had **all** that negative talk coming from the society he **lived** in: Being told **no** because of the colour of his **skin**. It's just bonkers that **anyone** would *choose* to **think** that way towards a fellow **human being**. **Arthur's** monkey chatter must have been **crazy** loud with all that going on outside his **head**.

But **Arthur** stood tall and carried on, he **used** what he had:

A desire to **play** tennis, coupled with,

determination and **downright** stubborn *intelligence*

which no one could **overturn**.

He succeeded in his **life** and in doing so touched the lives of **everyone**. Even when facing **adversity** and his life got upturned by illness he just '**used what he had**' once again by **choosing** to use **his** illness as a tool to educate his *fellow man*.

What a wonderous, talented human he was.

It makes me swell with pride to know that such important ripples of change can emanate from the actions of just one person and alter the future for everyone.

Oh blasssst.

All this chat and we have lost our Hero, he definitely went into the school gates for I heard the extremely loud lollipop lady shout:

'Goood Moooorning Vinnnnnie'.

But where oh where can he be now??

Such a large building I fear we may have missed our opportunity to see if he really can use what he has.

Reader, you really are the handiest of peoples to have about!

Of course, let US try Mr Winterbottom's classroom first.

Up the stairs we shimmy…. Shimmy……shmmmmmmy… mcshimmmmmy shim shim…….

There, there is the classroom door, it is slightly ajar.

"Goooooooooooood morning.........."

Mr Winterbottom's voice sounded extra loud and boomy in the empty classroom as he greeted Vinnie.

"Put your coat and bag on the peg and then take a seat at that table over there."

Mr Winterbottom points to the desk closest to his own large desk which is densely covered in exercise books.

Vinnie moves to the pegs and places his coat upon his.

He notices that his hands are a little sweaty and his heart rate is going faster than normal.

The Egolian inside of him is working extra hard to create feelings of failure and negativity.

Any feelings of confidence in this task Vinnie may have had at home have since melted away.

Images of an angry mum and no Edgebox until Christmas fill his mind.

"Earth to Vinnie."

The sound of Mr Winterbottom's voice makes Vinnie jump slightly.

"Sit here".

Vinnie moves towards the table being indicated again by the irritated teacher.

The chair scrapes across the floor making a strangled screaming sound as Vinnie pulls it out. He plonks his bum on it and places his legs under the desk.

Helen, the teaching assistant has just walked into the room carrying a large wodge of laminated sheets. She sits at a table near Vinnie and proceeds to cut stuff out.

In front of Vinnie is a piece of paper – there are sections marked out indicating that Vinnie should create a story outline for his piece of writing.

The story he will be expected to start and finish in the lesson later that morning.

A story which involves a time slip between the present and the past.

It is only a thin piece of ordinary paper, but it feels to Vinnie like a brick wall or a two-ton weight sitting in front of him – an impossible task.

He stares at the blank piece of paper and once again the imaginative area of his brain appears to have melted away.

In fact, the blasted monkey mind is replaying everything Vinnie has ever done wrong from the moment he had popped out of his mum, to this point. How is dropping a cornetto on his foot at age 6 even relevant right now?

Vinnie looks up, first at the clock, five whole minutes have passed already leaving him only a paltry twenty-five left, then he looks at Helen.

She has paused her cutting out and is glaring at Vinnie.

The urge to throw the piece of paper at her and storm from the classroom is strong. But the desire to have his controller back is stronger and from somewhere in Vinnies head the words of The Orb start to sneak through.

'Start Where You Are.'

Vinnie places his hands flat on the table in front of him.

He shuffles slightly in his seat adjusting his feet, so they are flat on the floor beneath him.

He softens his gaze – looking at his own hands – he cannot possibly close his eyes right now -the last thing he needs is for grumpy Helen to accuse him of having a nap!

His breathing slows and becomes shallow as he counts from one to ten, he does this four times before he realises the monkey has gone.

Instead, the words,

'Use what you have',

filter through to his consciousness.

He has a broken Edgebox controller and a game console he can't use.

The Egolian almost chuckles to itself as this thought enters Vinnie's mind, for Brenda mistakenly believes Vinnie is dwelling on his misfortune.

But Vinnie is not focusing on what he doesn't have – in fact,
quite the opposite.

He is using what he does have, granted it is an unfortunate situation bought about by his own lousy temper and a shocking aim which shattered the Edgebox controller beyond repair.

But he is drawing this situation in the first box on his piece of paper and adding a brief description beneath it.

In doing so, his imagination fires up. The next box he draws a strange combination type padlock appearing where the controller hit and smashed. It is there among the smashed remnants of the controller.

The character, a tall skinny boy of about 12, picks it up and fiddles with the numbers upon it. They stop at 0000. The boy presses the top of the padlock, it opens and suddenly woooooosh – a doorway has appeared on a nearby wall. The character is sucked into it without a moment to spare.

Vinnie smiles to himself as he draws the character being sucked into the doorway – a mad expression upon its face and a scared parp emitting from its trousers.

He has done it. He has actually drawn the beginning of the story.

Looking up at the clock he has 10 minutes left to complete it.

The next story box shows the boy coming out through the other side of the door and into a different age, dinosaurs are roaming around. The boy has a frightened startled look upon his face as he tries to go back through the door, but it won't open. The door is locked!

It has upon it the combination padlock that initially opened the doorway. It is locked at 0000.

The frightened boy is faffing with the lock terrified he may be spotted by a pterodactyl flying overhead. He randomly enters the numbers 1889 into the lock causing the door to pop open slightly; the boy opens it.

Stepping through the door he now finds himself in Victorian England. The streets are grubby, and people rush past, some are dressed in finery and others scruffy.

A small boy holds up a newspaper with the headline *'Ripper Strikes Again'*.

Vinnie's imagination is on fire right now. He remembers covering Victorian England in school last year and all the year 5 kids had to dress up in Victorian school clothes. His mum cut up some of his older school clothes, making them grubby and Vinnie wore those to school with a flat cap his grandad gave him.

Vinnie smiles to himself at the memory, for that day was also a school trip day.

Vinnie loves school trips especially the coach ride as he always manages to sit next to Alfie, and they chat and laugh all the way to the school trip destination.

Last year, dressed as Victorian school kids they went to a Ragged School museum and the teachers were really bossy – more than Helen is, although Vinnie suspects she is so old she must have been a kid at the raggedy school for real.

Vinnie stops daydreaming to see Helen looking at him strangely.

He realises he had stopped writing and had been smiling to himself about Helen being a small child and being bossed about by a strict Victorian teacher.

Vinnie quickly glances back to his page. He remembers Jack the Ripper from the London Dungeon experience his parents took him to earlier this year. Putting that in the story will be awesome as they still don't know who he was.

Vinnie has decided that his storyboard will have the characters magic door open out onto the hiding place of 'Jack' and the mystery is solved making the headlines in the papers read 'Twelve-year-old boy smarter than entire London Police Force.'

Smiling to himself as he finishes the last area of the storyboard, Vinnie looks up. It is just coming up to 8.45 am and all the kids will be coming into the class very soon.

"Helen, please can I go to the toilet?"

Vinnie asks as Helen is wrestling with a sheet of partially laminated paper which has got itself wedged in the laminating machine.

"Only if you have finished all your work".

The look on Helen's face demonstrating doubt that Vinnie has completed the task set.

"All done!"

Vinnie replies with a confident smile upon his face.

"Really??........"

Helen's face is shocked as she leans forward and does indeed see a fully completed storyboard.

"Oh – well yes then Vinnie off you go."

With that Vinnie jumps up and walks triumphantly to the boy's toilet just down the corridor, leaving Helen losing her fight with the laminator as it switches itself off still clutching the partially laminated work in its stubborn jaws.

Vinnies's face carries a broad smile,
his eyes are twinkling with the fresh feeling of success
as he saunters down the empty corridor towards the loo.

Brenda is desperately trying to force thoughts about failure into Vinnie's mind but to no avail.

This Hero is walking on air.

A short while later, after a very triumphant wee in which he managed to aim all of it into the urinal and none on the floor, walls, or his shoes Vinnie returns to the now full classroom.

Weaving his way through the throng of children sat at their desks, Vinnie finds his own and sits down oozing with confidence.

Mr Winterbottom quickly takes the register and then hands out the storyboards from the day before. There is no assembly today, allowing the class to get straight into the assessed writing.

Mr Winterbottom explains his expectations to the whole class.

"There is to be no talking during this lesson at all – you are to use all the skills you have learnt and show off in your writing."

He witters on......... but all Vinnie hears is......

"Blah blah... conjunctions, blah blah.....adverbs, blah blah blah prepositions, blah blah ......adverbials, blah blah blah relative clauses and blah blah blahdy blah ....nouns."

Vinnies's head is all of a spin.

Abverbwotnows?

Conjunction?
Isn't that an eye
infection or
summink??

Relativeclausewho?.

How on earth is he supposed to use all of this stuff in his story? He can't even remember what it all means, let alone how to use it.

The classroom around him fades away slightly as he is focused on the words whizzing around his head and the tight feeling in his stomach.

His mouth is dry, and he feels a little dizzy.

His head is filling with can not's and am nots.

Brenda is, of course, spinning with glee. Its fear of being mastered is all but washing away in the sea of doubt and fear.

It is now time for the class to write their stories. Helen hands out the story maps to the class and they settle down to write.

Vinnie looks around the classroom, everyone is writing their story.

Everyone but him.

His mind is once again blank.

He picks up his pencil from the table.

Brenda is willing him to lob it at Helen, that way he will be made to leave the class and away from this awful writing situation.

Vinnie stares at the pencil in his hand for a few seconds before moving his gaze to one corner of his piece of paper.

To the untrained eye of the teaching assistant and the teacher, Vinnie looks like he is concentrating on the story and is thinking about where to start.

Inside Vinnie is counting his breaths once again.

He looks at his storyboard and a small smile escapes his lips.

I don't have a clue what Mr WinterBUTTHOLE is talking about.........

....but I do know my story is the dog's doo dahs......

With that Vinnie picks up his pencil and starts to write.

As he writes, the story flows. It flows from his imagination, down his arm, through his hand into the pencil and on to the paper in front of him.

The more Vinnie relaxes into the story it allows his energy to flow and the better he feels.

Brenda on the other hand is feeling constricted, like it's a yoghurt tube being squeezed in the middle.

A short while later, Mr Winterbottom stands up.

"Right class, pencils down, I said PENCILS DOWN. Time to stop writing."

The whole class lets out a collective sigh of relief.

Helen walks around the room collecting all the written work and
storyboards.
It is break time and the class are let out into the playground, the entire
class walk down the stairs and out the door like a tsunami of relieved
children.

"How was it coming in early today, Vin?"

Alfie asks, fully aware that his friend had been dreading it all of yesterday.

"T'was all right, my story is awesome too.
If Mr WinterBUTThole isn't happy with it
I will actually walk out of this poopy da pants school
and never come back!"

Vinnie answers smiling as he does, confidence in his story shining through
the not altogether untrue threat.

They run off to join some other friends to play 'It', and before long,
the whistle for the end of break time is blown.

FWEEEEEEEEEEEETTTTT......

As the class return to their seats, Mr Winterbottom has an announcement.

**"Well, year 6.
I have had a quick look at the work
from our assessed write,
and there are a couple of stories
I would just like to share with you."**

The class look attentively at Mr Winterbottom, each child wondering if their story has been picked.

Vinnie doesn't.

He knows his won't be picked, it never is, except to be told what he had forgotten to do.

He is not really listening as the first story is reviewed, the class give the child a clap as their name is written on the 'Board of Excellence' (this a board in the classroom where the children who have given 100% effort have their names written for all to see).

"...next we have Vinnie's awesome time travelling story involving a combination lock....."

At the mention of his name Vinnie's heart beats superfast.

He can't believe he is being singled out for something good, it is most unusual, and he is not quite sure how to deal with it.

A small nervous smile spreads across his lips, and his face flushes a little warm.

He listens as Mr Winterbottom regales the class.

"........ Vinnie used verbs like investigate and admire. He chucked in the adverbial 'with a smile on his face', the pronouns 'he' and 'they' and topped it off some fantastic punctuation...."

Vinnie is completely amazed.

I did??

By relaxing into his writing and allowing it to flow naturally. It seems his brain had remembered all those things, even if it couldn't remember what they were called.

As Mr Winterbottom finishes singing Vinnie's praises, Helen walks back over to the board of excellence to write Vinnie's name upon it.

Vinnie is beaming,
his nervous smile has become a huge smile of pride.

When Helen walks past the teacher towards the board, something outstandingly crazy occurs.

Mr Winterbottom's chair slips from beneath him, he manages to steady it by grabbing the table stopping it falling completely. As he does, his foot accidentally catches Helen on the bottom.

Causing her to turn around, she clutches her left butt cheek whilst offering Mr Winterbottom one of her well used 'death stares'.

"Oh, my goodness me, sorry Helen."

Mr Winterbottom exclaims genuinely fearful for his life as the class behind him start to giggle at Helen grabbing her own bottom in shock.

Alfie turns to Vinnie.

"Gosh, Vin, I wish I had gone for a pee at break time. I completely forgot and I don't recon Mr Winterbottom will let me go now...."

By this point, Vinnie has a most curious of looks upon his face, a mix of wonder, disbelief, and amusement.

Alfie is bouncing up and down on the chair next to Vinnie, his hand aloft as he calls out.

"Helen, please may I go to the toilet, I forgot to go at break time."

Helen turns to Alfie, her face still carrying the 'Death Stare', which does indeed nearly make Alfie pee his actual pants.

"Alfie, you really should have gone at breaktime."

Vinnie rolls his eyes at a typical Helen response. Alfie had literally just told her that same thing.

Oh. Ma. Gowd. I can't believe she just said that.

Helen ushers Alfie out of the classroom and he scurries off as fast as he can.

"Quiet, Quiet......, **QUIET**."

Mr Winterbottom bellows at the class.

Causing everyone to stop with the giggling and focus on the next lesson, which is math.

Vinnie has a smile across his face.

Not a crazy joker style smile but a small smile of satisfaction.

This is indeed an exceedingly rare occurrence.

Alfie returns to the classroom, clearly relieved and whispers quietly to Vinnie.

"That was well close Vin,
I nearly peed myself especially when
Mr Winterbottom caught Helen's bum with his foot."

Even though Helen was nowhere near the boys, her almost superpower like hearing picked up on the whispering, and the mention of her name.

She turns to the boys, her face carrying a twisted irritated look – much like it always does.

"Shuuuuuuush."

Alfie stops immediately and shoots his gaze to Mr Winterbottom pretending he has no idea why Helen is shuuuushing him.

The next lesson whizzes by, Vinnie has never really struggled with math, and before long it is lunchtime.

Vinnie plays an almighty game of football with his friends and some of the year five kids. He scores an awesome hat trick and by some miracle, manages to remain in play the entire lunchtime.

His friends are well impressed.

"Wow Vin, you are like the man of the match or summink!!"

"Yeah Vin, you're well good! I reckon you could play for England."

The school day draws to a close and Vinnie has managed a full day without any strikes. He nearly got one in art when he swiped some paint off the other table.

But Vinnie's continued positive frame of mind caused him to react with an apology instead of an argument when Helen confronted him and as a result avoided the strike entirely.

The end of the day bell rings out, and Vinnie leaves the gates.

A familiar face is waiting for him.

"Nan!!"

His nan has come to babysit this evening so mum and dad can go out.

Vinnie hadn't even known she was coming as he excitedly tells her about the amazing story he wrote and all about his name on the board.

"...and then Mr Winterbutt... er sorry Mr Winterbottom accidentally kicked Helen up the bum and the whole class laughed......... I got man of the match at lunchtime scoring Three, THREE goals past Dean, and he is well good at goalie........."

Nan smiles warmly at him, listening attentively.

"Oh, Vinnie that is lovely to hear.
I tell you what, lets pop to the shop on the way home, I have a £5 note burning a hole in my pocket."

Vinnie looks worriedly at his nan's coat for signs of smoke.

"Nan, if it's on fire we need to put it out quick..."

Nan laughs gently as she responds.

"Oh no Vin, it means we need to go spend it.....
an old-fashioned turn of phrase I imagine now..."

Vinnies eyes light up like car headlights as Nan explains. He just cannot
believe the course of events from today.

It is almost the same as his re-imagined day yesterday.

Vinnie ponders the situation as he walks to the shop with his nan.

How is this even a thing?

Is this possible?

Can my thoughts really be that powerful?

Nans do say daft things!
Five-pound notes on fire!!

Sometime later, with pockets full of sweets and some fizzy pop in hand Vinnie and his nan get home.

"Mum, Mum, muuuuuuum!!"

Vinnie calls out as soon as they walk through the front door.

"Hey Vin, you look happy!"

Responds mum as she walks towards them, stopping briefly to give her mum a hug and a kiss.

"Vinnie has some awesome news for you."

Nan tells Vinnie's mum; she is nearly as thrilled about it as Vinnie is.

Vinnie's eyes are alive with excitement as he tells his mum about this most spectacular of days, barely stopping for breath as he does!

"Well, I wrote an awesome story with dinosaurs, jack ripper a time-travelling lock and a super clever boy, Winterbutthole......"

"Vinnie, You really shouldn't call him that."

Interrupts mum, doing a bit of Mumming.

"Oh, all right.......*Mr Winterbottom*......"

Vinnie responds, pausing briefly while his brain catches up to where he had got to in his retelling of this most awesome of days.

"..... Erm......yeah..... Well, then he read the story out to the class as one of the best stories and Helen put my name on the Board of Excellence!"

Mum has a smile on her face that matches Vinnies,
as she swoops in for a hug.

"What's going on here? Oh, hi Nan."

Ben asks as he walks down the stairs surprised to greet his nan.

"Vinnie has done super well in his English today".

Mum tells him.

Ben looks momentarily surprised towards Vinnie before responding.

"Well done Vin."

He goes in for a hug too, but Vinnie sticks his arm out to thwart the attempt at brotherly love.

"Ewwwwwwwwwww. gerrrosss me!!"

Vinnie is off walking up the stairs quickly to avoid any more attempts from Ben to hug him.

The Orb is cowering on top of the wardrobe when Vinnie enters his bedroom.

A floofy assassin is on the bed.

Judging by the scratch marks on the side of the wardrobe has been trying to reach The Orb.

Taking a most catlike glance at Vinnie as he walks in.

It decides to mooch off down the stairs in search of some treats from the human 'nan'.

Vinnie closes the door behind the cat as he turns to The Orb.

"Best day everrrrrrr!"

He exclaims excitedly, carrying on with vigour as The Orb floats slowly down from the wardrobe.

It comes to rest on the bed next to Vinnie.

"I wrote the best story in the whole wide world,
played awesome football.
Then I got all these sweeties and pop from Nan."

With that Vinnie takes a large swig of fizzy orange. Pauses, before letting rip with an almighty....

"Buuuuuuuuurrrrrrrrrrrrrrrrrrrrrrrrrrrrrrrrrp"

The Orb took the smelly orange burp full-on in its face, Vinnie giggles as The Orb turns slightly green in response.

"Great news Hero!"

The Orb congratulates the smiling boy.

"The positive vibes emanating from you right now are the most powerful I have felt from you.

More good things are certainly on their way!"

Vinnie sits on the bed, smiling and relishing the positivity swirling around in his head, The Orbs words of encouragement making him feel light as air.

"Hero, now is a good time to close your eyes and listen."

Vinnie looks towards The Orb, slightly confused by this.

"But why? I am feeling amazing, no angry feelings or monkeys to sort out now, Orby McOrbbutt......."

Choosing to ignore the 'butt' element to its nickname, The Orb explains.

"Hero, these wonderful feelings that you are experiencing should be embraced.

By closing your eyes and focusing on these feelings you can in fact supercharge them!"

The Orb transforms into the headphones and attaches itself to Vinnies ears. Vinnie sighs and closes his eyes.

"......golden yellow........."

"......mmmm.......floating..."

A few minutes pass before The Orb gently whisps off Vinnie's head as though it was made of a soft candy floss fog.

"Oh, my days Orb. I feel like I could take on the world, like I am a weightless superhero!!"

With that, Vinnie hops off the bed and practically floats down the stairs.

Vinnie's evening continued along its positive way.

Mum and Dad went out and Vinnie and Ben spent a lovely evening with their Nan.

She popped their favourite pizzas in the oven for dinner and then they played a board game together.

Nan loves a board game, and they chose 'The Game of Life' to play this evening.

An awesome game where you have to move through the board with a tiny car shaped counter, entering different stages of life – education, marriage, babies (maybe!), collecting money as they do and choosing career paths the game ends with retirement in either a millionaire's mansion or a retirement home depending on how well the route through life went.

Vinnie didn't win.

Ben did.

Now ordinarily this would not have been well received. Ordinarily this would have made Vinnie see red and stomp around the house or worse still pin Ben down and fart on his head.

But not tonight.

Tonight, Vinnie is floating on a cloud of confidence.

Ben and Nan are both surprised and to be honest, loving this 'new' Vinnie.

Ben is put to bed and Vinnie and Nan watch an animal wildlife show on the tv. Vinnie had forgotten how much he enjoyed watching tv with his nan.

Time for bed and this evening Vinnie writes down **two** things he is grateful for.

He drifts off to sleep with a smile on his face as The Orb has a soft contented glow on top of the wardrobe.

"When I wake up I will feel energised and excited for the day ahead."

There is an energy about the room, like a massive hug from someone special – warm, safe, loved.

Well, I never! Well, I did! Our **Hero** only went and **did** it!

What a *wondrous* **day** it has been - *recognition* for **great** work, sweets from the

Nan and no **farts** on a little brother's head.

The Orb may **not** be as green as it is *cabbage* looking after **all!!**

These **positive** energy **vibes** are most *exciting* - I wonder *what else* they will

manifest, *exciting* times ahead dear Reader, oh **yes** exciting times *ahead!*

I **do** believe this *day* is my **favourite** yet –

Tiiiiiiime for a ryyyyyyme!

Rhyme time, yes yes, **rhyme** time..

Our Hero's story was the best,
It passed the teachers writing test.
By calming his monkey mind
The words, our Hero, he did find.

The teacher then read out the work,
Causing the class to go berserk.
When he slipped in his teacher chair,
And kicked the assistant in her derriere!

The fun did not end there you see,
For Alfie, he did need to pee.
Our Hero's in shock as the day unfolds,
For it is the day he had retold.

Man of the Match, he was declared,
During football not a goal was spared.
The Nan, she met him after school,
Vinnie is smiling like a fool.

Nan declares 'my pockets on fire',
It is the money, Vinnie did desire.
Sweets and pop were bought from the store,
lollipops and chocs galore.

A day so wonderous was shared,
to mum as she just stood and stared.
So proud and happy she did feel,
as she went out for her evening meal.

Sit still a while, The Orb directed,
the positive energy was collected.
It flowed down through our Hero's chair,
feel like a superhero! He did declare.

Some TV is had, with Nan by his side,
bedtime is soon here tiredness it cannot hide.
Two things?! Oh, what a grateful day,
I hope this positivity will stay.

Reader, Reader go and peek,
a copy of the story, I did sneak,
from the class into the book,
It's over there, go take a look.

In this door is old England. Lots of people some are well scruffy.

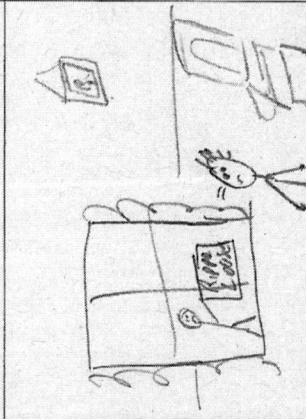

Dinosaurs everyhere. boy is stuck. Turns lock and it goes to 1889.

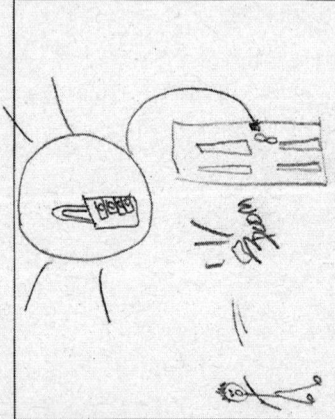

Controller smashes and lock appears. Makes a door and boy walks in.

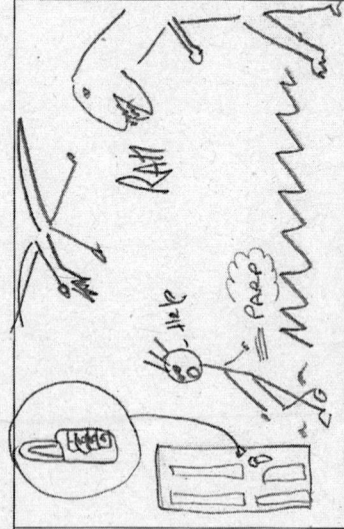

Everyone now thinks that the boy is cleverer than all the police. BooYah.

Realises he is in Jacks room and catches him.

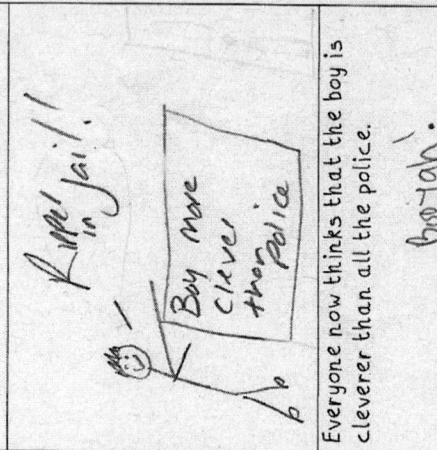

Jack the ripper is on the lose. Boy is in a room looking out at the street.

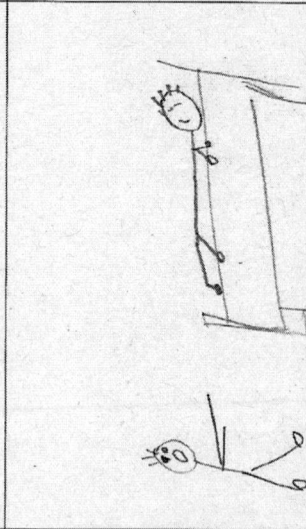

Super Charge Positive Vibes

When feeling good, expand the postive vibes by sitting still.

Pop a smile on your face.

Enjoy the postive feelings as they wash over you like a soft cloud or warm waterfall.

Use the meditation if you like.

Leaves you feeling like a super hero!

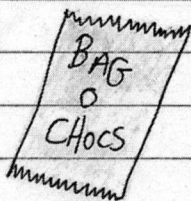

Thursday.

Good morning **Reader** of the words.

Good *mornings* **indeed!**

The *positive vibes* **generated** from yesterday still tingle within my very **self**, do *you* feel them **too?**

The Orb's **harnessing** of the *positivity* was a stroke of genius, tingle, tingle, tingle I *go!*

Now today is a further **school** *day*. I remember **you** saying there are **five** of those in total until the week of ends - **not** long now!!

I am *super* excited to **see** what awaits **us** on a week of ends. **Yes,** *you* are right *dear* Reader.

We must not chat **too** long for I am interested in **how** our **Hero** is this *morning*.

Let **us** *sneak in,* I may *be* **able** to peek in at **his** dreams to see *if* there is an improvement on the **empty** void of **nothingness**.

Reader. **Reader,** *something* is **not** quite **correct.** As WE approach our **Hero's bedroom**.

I hear *music!*

But it is *barely* **morning.** This is most odd.

We must **venture** in and find out what has *taken over* this place.

"I'm happy......"
Clap along if you feel like a room without a roof..."

Vinnie is at that very moment standing on his freshly made bed and wiggling his pyjama clad bottom in The Orbs direction as he sings along to some music emanating from his phone.

".........because I'm happy....
Clap along if you know what happiness is to you......"

The Orb is spinning round the light shade as it sings with Vinnie. Its glow is so bright it looks like the sun has shrunk and appeared in Vinnie's bedroom.

The floofy cat has managed to sneak in
and is watching in awe as The Orb spins and spins.

It's head whizzing round and round as it tries to follow The Orb.

Feeling like it has just been for a spin on a Waltzer ride
at a fairground, the floofy cat leaves the room,
to find a pair of shoes to vomit into.

"Hey Orby. I feel amazing this morning.
Like I can take on the world!!"

Vinnie declares as he leaps off the bed expertly landing on both feet.
He continues the bottom wiggle dance in the middle of the room.

Brenda is not feeling so clever.

The Egolian is at that very moment trying with all its might
to push some worries up from the pit of Vinnie's stomach,
with such pressure it has made itself look like a constipated raisin.

Suddenly Dad appears at the doorway rubbing his eyes, he is so sleepy that
he mistakes The Orb for the ceiling light.

He tries a couple of times to switch the light off,
muttering something about electricity not being free.

Before giving up and turning his attention to Vinnie.

"Blimey Vin. You're full of beans this morning –
    best turn that down so you don't wake Ben.
    It's not quite time for him to be up.."

He smiles at Vinnie as he closes the door behind him. Vinnie can hear him
mumbling to himself about having to get an electrician round to sort out
that light as he tiptoes downstairs, narrowly avoiding the Floofy cat as he
does.

Vinnie switches his phone off as plonks his bum back on the bed letting out
a happy sigh.

Brenda tries to use this opportunity to force some feelings of anxiety upon Vinnie, it is trying to make him feel worried about the near-miss with Dad and The Orb.

But Vinnie is in too much of a positive frame of mind to feel that anxiety, he turns his attention to The Orb as it speaks to him.

" Oh Hero, indeed this day has such a wonderous feel about it, positive energy is flowing.

Hero, did you realise that you have stopped dwelling on the feelings of lack?

You have not mentioned the controller situation for aaaaaaaages!"

Vinnie sits for a moment pondering The Orb's words.

"Ya know what Orb..... I hadn't even realised. I had such a good day yesterday, and nan coming over I had completely forgotten all about the Edgebox.

Tell ya what tho, I will make sure Ben doesn't win at the board game again — he was just well lucky......"

With that, Vinnie leaves the room humming the tune to himself as he wanders downstairs in search of some breakfast. Walking into the kitchen, still humming to himself, Vinnie stops abruptly when he finds both his mum and dad in there.

They were talking in hushed, quiet voices which suddenly stopped as Vinnie entered. He looks at them quizzically.

"Oh! Morning................"

Dad stands up from the table, shooting mum a strange, almost sad look as he does.

"Let's chat again later – when I am in from work."

He touches mums' hand gently before turning to Vinnie. His expression is back to normal, but a strange electric-like energy hangs in the air.

"Thanks for turning the music off Vin. Well done on yesterday's writing thingy - keep up the good work. Be nice to Ben and I will see you later."

With that he walks out the room to get ready for work, leaving mum sipping her coffee and staring into her phone. Vinnie feels uneasy like something is amiss, but he can't figure it out.

Brenda is ecstatic. There is now room to feed this energy.

Worry and anxiety start filling Vinnies body, pushing up into his mind. The song from earlier replaced with anxious thoughts.

What's going on? What did I do now? Is Nan ok? Where's the cat? My tummy feels like I need a big fart.... Can't fart now, mum will probably shout at me....

Vinnies's thoughts are interrupted by the sound of mum blowing her nose on a piece of kitchen roll.

Has she been crying??

Mum stands up from the table and heads for the door.

"Mum...are you......"

Vinnie tries to talk to her but is interrupted mid-sentence.

"..... not now Vin, just get ready for school, yeah......."

Vinnie notices that her eyes are blotchy as she leaves the kitchen and he is left alone.

Alone with his thoughts, and Brenda.

The Egolian is spinning around and gaining much momentum with this negative energy.

Even the sight of his favourite cereal still being in the cupboard was not enough to lift Vinnie's spirits.

A heavy cloud of confusion hangs over Vinnie as he slowly eats his breakfast. Thoughts continue to circle his mind as he tries to understand what he had just walked in to.

They have been arguing again.

They went out last night. I thought that was a good thing.

The cat had better not have puked on my school shoes again.

Vinnie is unable to finish his breakfast, knots in his stomach won't allow him. He abandons the half-eaten cereal, discarding his bowl on the table as he wanders out the kitchen.

Dad is in the hallway getting ready to leave for work,
an angry expression upon his face.
He is using some wipes to violently clean cat vomit
from the side of his expensive work shoes.

He doesn't notice Vinnie walking down the hallway, and Vinnie decides that
now is probably not the best time to ask him what is going on.

So, he continues up the stairs and into his bedroom.

"dummm de dummmmm dum dum dum.......
............happy........
dee deee de deeee dum dummmm dum dum..."

Vinnie walks in to find The Orb still humming and singing the song from
earlier – which to Vinnie, now feels like a lifetime ago.

He plonks himself on his bed and sits staring into space.

"Hero, whatever is wrong?
Your positive glow has positively disappeared..."

Vinnie sighs loudly before turning to The Orb to explain.

"Mum and dad are up to something;
they never tell me anything...... It's like they think I am
stupid and don't notice.
They think they are good actors, but they are rubbish.
I just don't know what is going on.
                    It pees me right off.."

With that, Vinnie gets off the bed to find his school clothes. The Orb hovers nearby.

"Hero, it is worth remembering that in any situation you have the power to choose how you feel.

Even if an external situation is out of your control, you have the choice about how it makes you feel."

Vinnie looks at The Orb, a quizzical expression on his face as he tugs on his school trousers and tucks in his shirt and gets ready for school.

"You aren't helping at all. How can I control how I feel?
It just happens.
It is nothing to do with me.
This week is so confusing.
I wish you had never appeared.
I wish I had never thrown my stupid controller.
All of this rubbish wouldn't be happening if I hadn't done that.

It's all my stupid fault."

With that, Vinnie leaves the room before The Orb has a chance to respond. The Orb watches Vinnie from the window as he heads off to school.

Walking slowly like the weight of the world is on his shoulders.

As Vinnie approaches the school gates, a familiar face catches sight of him.

"Vin, Vin, VIN!"

Vinnie carries on pretending not to see his friend Alfie.

He is too caught up in his own head to be bothered with people right now.

The Egolian in Vinnie is feeling a huge sigh of relief, that was close. Especially with that song this morning, that really had silenced the Egolian, if only for a short while.

Brenda is stirring up some corkers of negative energy.

Vinnie ignoring Alfie was the manifestation of that negative energy.

If the boy doesn't even want to play with his friends he is well and truly in the Egolians negative energy trap.

Brenda just needs to keep him there.

"Vinnie............ Vinnie....... VINNNIE...."

Now in the classroom and Mr Winterbottom is taking the class register.

Vinnie doesn't hear his name being called as his thoughts are still focused on home.

Maybe I should ask Nan what is going on.......

No point asking Ben, he such a div, won't know anything.

Wish the cat had puked on Ben's shoes and not dads.

Mr Winterbottom tries again.

"Earth to VINNNNIIIIEEEEEEE....."

Helen is making her way across the classroom to give Vinnie a poke. Alfie bashes Vinnie gently with his elbow which suddenly rouses Vinnie from the thoughts in his head.

"Huh..??"

A surprised Vinnie looks up at the teacher.

Stopping Helen in her tracks, she offers Vinnie a death stare.

Mr Winterbottom continues.

**"Nice of you to join us, Vinnie.
Remember when your name is Called you say,
'Yes' not 'Huh?!' you are not a blithering idiot….."**

The class sniggers as Mr Winterbottom continues taking the rest of the register.

Helen returns to her seat keeping one eye on Vinnie.

Vinnie is seething.

Bubbles of rage are trickling under the surface of his skin.

The Egolian is ecstatic.

Alfie is worried for his friend; he can see something is wrong.

Vinnie is trying hard to control the thoughts in his head, his hands are gripped into tight little fists.

He happens to glance over at Helen.

She is looking right at him, she silently shakes her head,
in that annoying manner that adults do to show their disappointment in you.

Vinnie sees her let out a big sigh as she turns her attention back to the teacher, who has now moved on to teaching as though nothing had just happened.

Vinnie can still hear the giggles of the classroom echoing around his head with the words 'blithering idiot' spinning about.

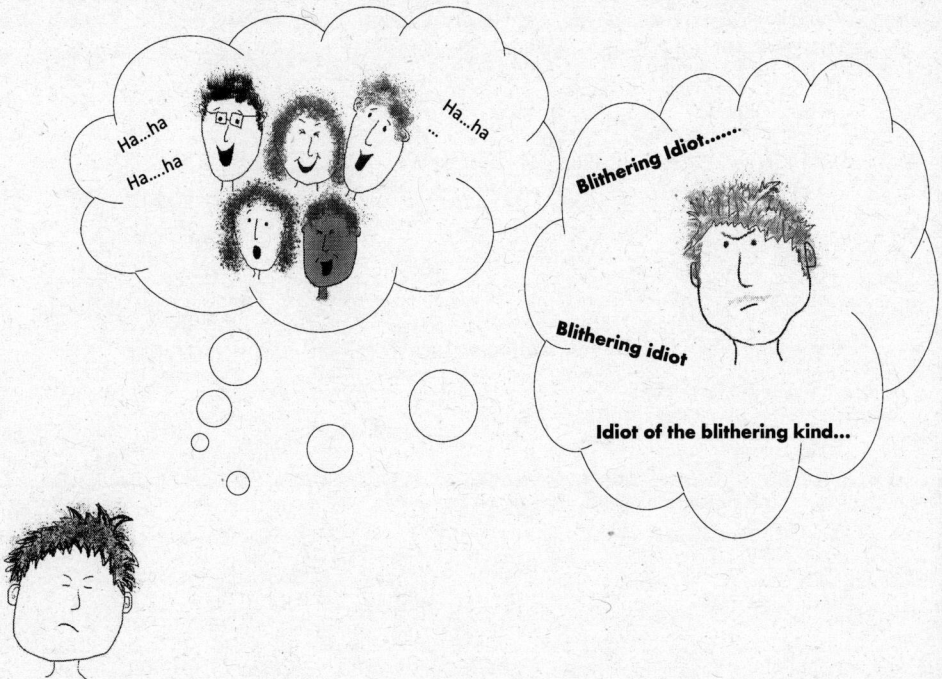

The Egolian within him is spinning itself into a frenzy.

Vinnie's self-control is hanging on by a thread.

It lets forth one final surge of *blithering idiot.*

Suddenly Vinnie stands up, eyes angry and fist still clenched, he glares at the teacher.

His friend, Alfie tries to tug him back down into his seat.

But the sound of the chair scraping on the floor has caused the teacher to stop his teaching,

His attention turns towards Vinnie, just as Vinnie loses it completely.

"You're the blithering IDIOT!!"

Vinnie shouts at the stunned teacher. The whole class is shocked into stillness as they watch to see what will unfold.

Mr Winterbottom uses his calm but angry teacher voice.

**"Vinnie, I suggest you sit down right now,
Sit down now and all you will get is a strike,
carry on and I will send you to Mrs Teague.
SIT DOWN."**

The entire class is at this very moment, collectively holding their breath to see what will happen next. Mr Winterbottom and Vinnie are caught in a sort of staring competition.

Alfie is willing his friend to sit down; this is not good.

He is worried that this friend will be moved from his seat, and he will end up having Harry seated next to him.

This is a concern as Harry is well known as a bit of a nose picker, and worse still, wipes the crusty bogeys under the table.

Vinnie and Mr Winterbottom continue to stare at each other.

Only seconds have passed but to the class, it feels like ages.

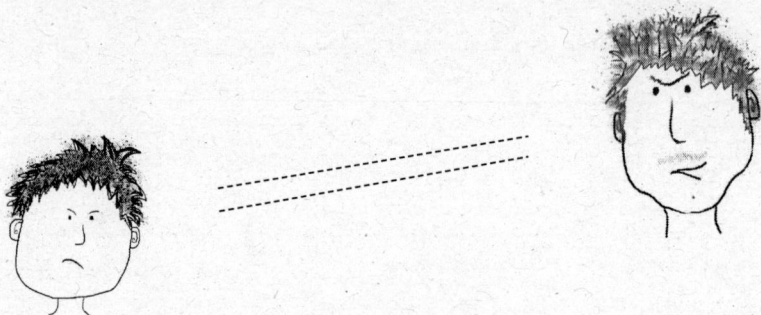

Out of the corner of his eye, Vinnie sees Helen get up and walk towards the board to place a strike against Vinnie's name.

At that very moment, the Egolian in Vinnie squeezes out one enormous fart like cloud of angry vibes.

Something takes over Vinnie.

Feelings of rage and indignation bubble to the surface and spill out from Vinnie's mouth.

"NO! I will not SIT DOWN. YOU sit down Mr Winter BUTThole ugly faced poo bum IDIOT."

As the words spill from Vinnie's mouth the entire classroom of children, the teaching assistant and the teacher are stunned.

It is as though they are frozen in time, mouths agape as their collective brains try to comprehend the angry boy's outburst.

Suddenly a pencil whizzes through the air.

It whacks Mr Winterbottom smack bang in the middle of his chest, instantly propelling him into action.

He marches across the classroom.

"OUT..... GET OUT OF THE CLASSROOM NOW......."

Mr Winterbottom is now stood next to Vinnie, pointing towards the door as his angry voice booms around the classroom.

The anger which had taken over Vinnie begins to fade. He can see the whole class attention is on him.

Vinnie stares silently at the angry teacher. Unsure of how to handle this situation.

I don't know how to handle this.

Mr Winterbottom misinterprets Vinnie's hesitation as disobedience, so he repeats his angry instruction.

"I said OUT. LEAVE the classroom. Helen will walk you to Mrs Teague. NOW OUT...."

With that Helen walks across the classroom.

Vinnie turns towards the door and walks through it as Helen reaches his side.

Mr Winterbottom's voice can be heard directing the class back to the lesson as Vinnie and Helen walk silently towards the headteacher's office.

Mrs Teague is finishing up some writing as they walk in.

Helen motions to Vinnie to sit down on the chair as she explains to the headteacher the reason for their presence.

"blah blah........... shouted at the teacher..........
Blah blah......... wouldn't sit down........
Blah blah...... threw a pencil......
Blah blah......"

A silence fills the small room as Helen finishes her recount.

The room feels claustrophobic as Vinnie waits for the headteacher to respond.

"Well, Vinnie. What a disappointing turn of events Helen has just described.
And after such a super day yesterday.

I am extremely disappointed in you.

Thank you for bringing Vinnie to me Helen,
you may now return to class."

With that, the sour-faced teaching assistant turns out of the Headteachers office and heads back to class.

Vinnie and Mrs Teague are alone.

She does that 'I am super disappointed' look at Vinnie.

"Well Vinnie,
do you want to tell me what just happened??"

Mrs Teague looks at Vinnie.

He looks back at her – unwilling to talk.

The headteacher lets out a sigh as she picks up the phone on her desk and dials. After a short silence, the phone is answered on the other end.

"Hello, this is Mrs Teague from the school,
about Vinnie..... No, don't worry he is not
hurt I am sorry I understand you are at work.....
yes I appreciate that......
Vinnie has behaved in the most unacceptable of manners
well, he shouted abuse at the teacher and threw a pencil
across the class and it hit the teacher.......... Well, no, I don't know the reasons
why. Vinnie is yet to talk to me........ hmmmm..... Yes, I am sure there is a reason
for it........ even so, we feel it is best if Vinnie stays with me today and I will need
to see you when you come to pick him up........ we need him to understand that
this behaviour will not be tolerated......   Yes, that is fine. I will see you then.
Goodbye......"

Vinnie sits in shock as the magnitude of what has just happened starts to sink in.

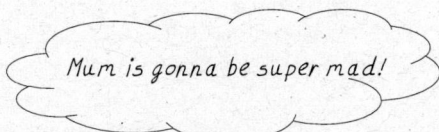

The entire day drags heavily along, like an elephant with an itchy butt.
Hours and hours pass in the headteacher's room where Vinnie must remain.

Work is given to him from Mr Winterbottom and every so often the
headteacher tries to coax Vinnie to talk about the morning's events.

Vinnie is in such a dark place about the whole incident,
his mouth is shut tight like a clam.

It's like the morning's outburst used up all his words and his energy.
The end of the school day is finally here, and a flustered looking mum
appears at the headteacher's door.

The headteacher motions for mum to sit down then
mum again about the 'incident'.

"Well, as I said earlier. It just seemed to come out of nowhere,
from what Helen has said. Vinnie just lost his temper with
Mr Winterbottom and was shouting and throwing things.
I have had no explanation from Vinnie at all today.
Is everything alright at home?"

There is a pause as Mrs Teague allows mum to register what she has been
told. Mum gaze briefly flicks to Vinnie. A weary look across her face.

"Erm, No. No, there is nothing different at
home. I really don't understand what would
have caused this outburst. Vinnie, what do
you have to say for yourself??"

There is a silence in the room as both the headteacher and mum cast their
attention to Vinnie.

The Egolian inside him springs into action.

Causing a rise in feelings of disbelief and unfairness to bubble up to the surface. Vinnie stands up and turning towards the two adults, chooses this moment to speak.

"MR WINTERBOTTOM STARTED IT. HE CALLED ME AN IDIOT AND THE WHOLE CLASS LAUGHED........."

Mrs Teague has adopted a startled look upon her face as she responds to Vinnie's outburst.

"Well, this is the first I am hearing of this! Why don't you take Vinnie home and give him a chance to tell you what happened this morning? I will pop down to class and see what Mr Winterbottom has to say about it. Vinnie, I want you to come to school tomorrow ready to have a good day. Go home and have a good night's sleep. Tomorrow is another day!"

Mum and Vinnie leave the headteachers office, they pop to Ben's class to pick him up and then wander through the school gates.

Ben is full of questions from today as he couldn't see Vinnie at lunchtime and some older kids had filled him in with the morning's events.

"Vinnie – didn't see you at lunch today,
Tom from your class said you nearly blinded the
teacher with a pencil and the police were nearly
called to take you away!!"

Vinnie looks at Ben as though he is a walking turd.

"Oh, my Gawd, you're such a doofus and Tom
can just do one......."

Vinnie leans over and gives Ben a shove as he responds.

This act touched a nerve with mum.

In fact, the two boys may have finally got on that infamous 'last nerve' that
mum is often referring to.

"OK – THAT IS IT!!!!   When we get home, Ben you are
To put the tv on in the lounge and stay far away from
Vinnie.   And as for you Vin....... You can go straight
Upstairs and stay in your room until dinner......and
Vinnie..... you can kiss goodbye to that Edgebox controller.... You will be
lucky if you get one for next Christmas at this rate.....!!"

Vinnie just cannot believe how terrible this day has turned – it started with
a song and has ended like an overflowing cesspit of poop.

"But muuuuum......"
                        none of this even MY fault.

                        It's all Mr WinterBUTTfaces fault..."

He tries to fight his corner and explain but Mum is having none of it.

She is pretending not to hear Vinnie as she walks determinedly ahead,
leaving the two boys to walk the last bit, a few paces behind.

Vinnie glares angrily at his brother as though he is trying to stab his brain
with invisible daggers.

Before long, the unhappy trio reach the front door.
Both boys enter and dump their coats on the floor of the porch, Ben
disappears to the living room. Mum lets out a large sigh as she hangs up
the coats and heads to the kitchen.

                Vinnie follows her into the kitchen.

                        "Mum, you didn't mean that about the
                        Edgebox controller did you?? You said I
could have it sooner..... you said that because I had made my bed
and been working hard I could have it..... you said...."

Vinnie stops and stares at mum waiting for a response.

She pauses briefly and then turns towards Vinnie.

"Seriously Vin, you shouted at the teacher,
and threw a pencil.... Then you refused to leave the class,
and had to be escorted to Mrs Teague's office.
Where you then refused to speak for the whole
Day. So, NO ... you cannot have the blasted controller..."

The rage felt earlier bubbles up in Vinnie again.

"I HATE YOU....... YOU'RE JUST A LIAR
...YOU SAID I COULD......... LIAR LIAR....

I HATE YOU..."

Vinnies's outburst is suddenly interrupted by Dad.

He had come home early as he wasn't feeling well and had been lying on his
bed. He could hear the raised voices and had decided to come and see what
was going on.

"VINNIE, HOW DARE YOU SPEAK TO YOUR
MUM LIKE THAT........GET TO YOUR ROOM....."

Deciding not to argue, Vinnie leaves the kitchen and heads upstairs to his room.

Stopping briefly by the living room door to stick his tongue out at Ben.

'muuuuuuuummmm ....'

Vinnie legs it up the stairs quick sharpish not stopping until he reaches the santuary of his bedroom. He enters his bedroom to find the floofy cat on his pillow, cleaning its butt.

It looks up when Vinnie enters the room.

There is a change in the atmosphere.

Vinnie can feel that the room is different than when he had left for school this morning, kind of empty and ....cold.

He looks around for The Orb.

It is nowhere to be found.

The Egolian is feeling triumphant. With that blasted Orb gone this so-called Hero is now very much a zero.

This will keep things plodding along into the nothingness of the comfort zone.

The floofy cat has now jumped down on the floor, and is at that very moment doing a violent retching movement, like it is trying to turn itself inside out.

Did it eat the Orb?

Vinnie watches transfixed.

One final violent retch from the cat achieving nothing apart from the waft of a silent stinky cat food fart from its fluffy butt, it leaves the room in search of somewhere soft to lay.

Now completely alone, Vinnie is feeling a deeply confused cocktail of emotions, angry, sad, scared, betrayed.

He is caught between wanting to throw stuff out of his windows and lie on the bed crying.

With nothing to do in his room he lies on the bed and watches the Iron Man movie.

It did not make him feel any better – sure it was funny in places but overall, he still felt like he was in a dark lonely place.

Even when he was called for dinner, he didn't go.

There were no feelings of hunger at all.

Mum and dad left him in his room, they had had enough of Vinnie and this day too.

Vinnie could hear them chatting at dinner, Ben was telling them all about some boring tosh and he could hear them laughing.

He was fairly sure he could even hear the cat sniggering too.

Ha haha...

Ha Ha....Ha!

Ha haaaa ha...

Purrrrrrrrpppp....

This made Vinnie feel even more distant, he put on another movie to pass the time, this one however he did not see to the end.

The day had exhausted him so much that he fell asleep.

Still in his school clothes. On top of his bed.

Dad looked in on him and decided to let him sleep.
Pulling the covers over his eldest son, he kissed him gently on the forehead,
feeling bad for shouting at him earlier.

Night vin, love u xx

Reader.... Oh, my **Dear** dear Reader of the words.....

What has *befallen* **our** Hero?

Such a morning of **positivity** *shattered* into a quagmire of **doom**.

Norman is twisting my **innards** and *making* me feel like I should **like** to *leave*

this place and **never** return. The **Orb** is *gone*, the **Hero** is defeated, the

day is lost.

I *fear* **not** even my rhyme will **spur** us on to a *day of tomorrows*.

The day began with a joyful tune,
But much had changed by the afternoon.
Let's try to see where it all went wrong,
From the moment they sang the happy song.

Downstairs in the kitchen, Vinnie did find,
Mum and dad with something to hide.
This made his tummy feel a bit tight,
Had they been having another fight?

The cat had vommed on dad's work shoe,
At least it wasn't a steaming poo.
Back in the bedroom, Vinnie is distracted,
Leaving for school his mind quite contracted.

He misses his name when the register is called,
The teacher makes him feel like a fool.
Vinnie stands up and shouts his distress,
His mind is a tangled angry mess.

Whizz... the pencil flies across the room,
Like a tiny missile of impending doom.
Helen marches the boy to the head,
He must stay there all day instead.

Mum arrives with a look of despair,
Vinnie is cross, this just isn't fair.
The walk home is thwarted with angry words,
No controller again? That's just absurd.

At home, the anger continues to flow,
vexed words with rude gestures in tow.
Our Hero is sent by dad to his room,
Why was he home from work so soon?

The bedroom is empty apart from the cat,
Who tried to throw up its guts on the mat.
The Orb has gone, no sign of it here,
Is that an Egolian I can hear cheer?

The dinner was eaten without Vinnie there,
It's like the family just don't care.
On the bed, he has fallen to sleep fully clothed,
Exhausted from what the day had bestowed.

No grateful things he did write down,
He sleeps with a face full of frown.
Dad checked in and wished him goodnight,
Feeling sad from their earlier fight.

The Orb, I wonder where it has gone?
I hope it won't be gone too long.
I see in the notebook, some things it has left,
For the Hero to see so he won't be bereft.

Let us leave him something too,
A grateful thing to make him less blue.
Have a think Reader, what good did transpire?
Leave it in his notebook, it may help inspire.

I am *grateful* my pencil *did not* hit the teacher in the eye.

Friday.

Oh Reader, oh dear, dear Reader. *Yesterday* was the **worst** *day* ever.

I do **not** know *how* **our Hero** can come **back** *from* this **one**. Rude to the teacher, thrown out of **class**, a row with **mum** *and* dad.

Whatever will **he** do now?

Thank *goodness* **we** were able to *think of something* for our **Hero** *to be* grateful **for**. It **shows** *that* even in the *worst of times* there is always something **good** to reflect upon.

I *thought* he *should be* **grateful** that he didn't get the **teacher** in *the eye* with his pencil.

Let's hope *our Hero* feels **better** once he wakes *from* his *slumber*. A good night's **sleep** in *itself* can often **remove** the *shackles* cast from previous *day's* **events**.

That **Sean Swarmer** fella though.

Can **you** *imagine* being told at 13 that **you** *have weeks to live??*

The human **spirit** *never* fails to amaze me.

He *not only* **defied** all the odds *medically* but **then** went on to climb **all** the **mountains** of the **world** – the **power** to succeed is **not** defined by **what** others tell **you.**

Sean was told **he** was *going to die* by **doctors.**

There is *surely* **no** bleaker outcome *than* **that.**

It takes a **determination** to *see* beyond *that* **prognosis.**

And **ya** know **Reader**, Sean is just a *normal, everyday human* – **not** one *'superpower'* he **did not** get *bitten by a spider* **or** *fall into* a vat of something which *'changed'* him.

He is just a **regular guy.**

This *means* **Reader**, that this *power to overcome adversity* is within everyone. The **determination** to *succeed* is **not** a *physical* thing.

Afterall Sean's *illness* **did not** *leave* him **unscathed**.

He **lost** a **lung**.

That *did not* **stop** him - he *climbed* **mountains!**

To climb *mountains* **exposes** the *human* body to reduced oxygen as the air thins out the **higher** you climb.

Of **all** *the* things Sean *could* **have** done, **he** chose **one** of the things physically he would **be** *deemed* **least** likely to *succeed at* and **smashed it!**

What an inspiration!

Perhaps Sean's **story** can help *our* Hero *see* **beyond** *his* obstacles and *create* **his** *future*.

Let's move *into* the **bedroom**. Morning is *upon* us and I am **super** *keen* to see how this day **unfolds**.

Ah, *there* **he** is, *still* sleeping soundly under the **warmth** of his *duvet*.

Reader, this is **GOOD** *news*. I can see his **dreams!**

Despite the *awfulness* of **yesterday,** our Hero's **imagination** *appears* to have been *jumpstarted* by the weeks earlier good vibes.

In his **dream** he is playing **football** with his *friends*, there is much *jubilation* as he **scores** a *goal!*

See that *small smile* upon his *sleeping lips*. Hear the noise from his **bottom** as it releases a soft, *potent parp of success*.

This is a **good** dream.

Oh, *hang on* a roly mo, I *see*, in his **dream** a *figure approaching*.

It appears to be a grown-up, **but** there is *something* **most odd** about **them**.

Gaaaaahhhhhh, my eyes - my eyes!!

I will never *unsee* this monstrosity, for it is an *adult male* with a butt for a face.

Oh, the **horror!!**

I *believe* it to be Mr Winterbottom.

See **Reader**, *look* at our **Hero** now, a confused *frown* has appeared on his face.

Now a **smile** spreads across his lips.

BRRRRRIIIIIIINNNNGGGGGG!

Gaaaahhhh.... Saved *by* the bell.

I never **thought** I *would be* pleased to **hear** that **din.**

BRRRRRIIIIIIINNNNNGGGGGG!

The alarm ringing loudly next to Vinnie's bed causes the sleeping boy to spring up in shock.

"What the......'

He exclaims as he looks around the room.

BRRRRRIIIIIIINNNNNGGGGGG!

Vinnie reaches down and turns off the alarm.

A silence fills the air once again.

Rubbing the sleep from his eyes as the image of a human with a butt for a face disappears from his mind. It is replaced by a feeling of dread as the events from yesterday are recalled.

Vinnie sighs as he stands up.

Today is going to be hard.

A loud grumbling sound from his stomach reminds him that he fell asleep without any dinner the night before.

Stepping forward his foot catches on something on the floor, Vinnie looks down to find the notebook splayed open.

He treads on it with petulant disgust as he walks towards the door, his mission right now is food.

He is so hungry he could eat the cat.

The Egolian is also up and ready for the day ahead, it hasn't felt this strong all week.

The Orb has not shown itself, usually the annoyingly chirpy ball of positivity leaps upon the boy as soon as he wakes. But not this morning.

Brenda jumps straight to work,
     filling Vinnie's mind with anxiety for the day ahead.

As usual at this time of day, mum is in the kitchen when Vinnie walks in.

"Morning Vin, you must be starving.
          Let's have a better day today yeah?"

Brenda continues to create negative energy within Vinnie.

Vinnie has not forgotten the lost controller situation and it bubbles beneath the surface like a volcano of hate for his mum.

Finally, he opens his mouth to voice his obvious displeasure at the controller situation.

"Muuum....."

But Mum is not new and stops Vinnie in his tracks.

**"Vinnie, it is way too early for attitude.
And make sure you change your shirt and pants –
you can't go to school in yesterday's clothes."**

With that, she leaves the kitchen to enjoy her coffee in the living room.

Huh?! ○ ○ ○

Her last statement has left Vinnie confused. Brenda's negative energy had caused his focus from waking to immediately slip into feelings of lack, to think only of past events. His focus was so intune with what he did not have that he did not even notice that he was still wearing yesterday's school clothes.

At least it is Friday.

Vinnie ate his breakfast, or rather he wolfed his breakfast down in record time. He was starving. Wiping the excess milk from his mouth with the sleeve of his school shirt he wanders back up the stairs. With his belly tamed and his hangry vibes suppressed, his thoughts turn to The Orb as he re-enters his bedroom.

Where is that annoying glowing fartball anyway??

Brenda is not happy that the boy is looking for The Orb, it is however, most amused at the insulting new name the boy just coined for it.

Vinnie looks about the room, on top of the wardrobe, around the light shade, even poking about under the bed by moving his badminton racquet backwards and forwards to see if he could flick The Orb out from under it.

Nothing.

Maybe it was all just a weird dream??
Maybe there was never any fartball after all?

Vinnie's thoughts are interrupted as he once again spots the notebook on the floor slightly squashed from where he stood on it earlier. Picking it up he flicks through the pages.

> *So, it was real!! What is this??*
> *I don't remember writing this.*
> *I am grateful my pen didn't hit*
> *the teacher in the eye??*

Vinnie looks at the next page and finds one of the magic squares The Orb left. He takes his phone and scans it, the phone screen bursts into life and for a short while Vinnie's mind is on the movie playing on the screen, detailing Sean Swarmer and his awesome resolve.

The screen returns to normal as the short film ends.

Vinnie looks about the room expecting The Orb to have shown itself.

Nothing.

There is another square in the book and Vinnie is about to watch it when he realises the time.

He should get ready for school.

One more day then at least he can chill out at home and not have to see that annoying teacher.

Standing up, he turns around and makes his bed.
Instinctively, without thinking about it.

Brenda is not happy about this little revelation if the boy is now making his bed without The Orb reminding him, what other things from the fartball will impact its attempts to keep the boy within the 'Comfort Zone'?

Whilst the Egolian is trying to make sense of the bedmaking situation, Vinnie is sniffing the armpits of his shirt to determine if indeed he even needs to change for school.

Satisfied that he can get away with it he leaves the room and heads for the bathroom.

He readies himself on the loo for his morning poop, but nothing. He sits there a short while giving the occasional 'hummmmph' and a push causing his face to turn a radish red, but nothing not even a strangled parp escapes.

Giving up, Vinnie brushes his teeth, then heads to his room where he throws on his school shoes. One final glance around the room to see if The Orb has shown.

Nope.

Vinnie leaves the house, the sounds of his brother and mum chatting in the kitchen fill his ears as he closes the front door.

Vinnie has left in plenty of time, he needed to get out of the house it was doing his head in.

Dad had left early for work, at least that was something. Vinnie was in no mood for another lecture on how to behave, although he did vaguely recall a dream where his dad was stroking his head.

At least the walk to school early has also meant he doesn't have to put up with Ben this morning either, he is in no mood for that little vegturd and his rambling nonsense.

As he walks along the quiet street, Vinnies's mind moves from the stresses of his own family and begins to ponder the stresses of that Sean Swarmer fella he just watched on his phone.

Climbing mountains with one lung??
That is mad man.
I know for a fact I have two of them
and sometimes just running up the
Field at school is hard.

Vinnie's thoughts are interrupted as he approaches the school gates, he has arrived at the same time as Alfie. Alfie lives further away from the school than Vinnie and has to get the bus, he has to be early, the bus timetable makes it so.

"Vinnie.... Maaaaaate wasn't sure you would be in today. Mr Winterbottom was in a mood the rest of yesterday. You were well lucky to have been in with Mrs Teague."

Interesting perspective, as Vinnie hadn't felt lucky. He shrugs his shoulders at Alfie making no attempt at conversation for his mind now full of anxiety for the day ahead.

I bet today is going to feel like I Am climbing a mountain with no lungs...
Where was that Orb this morning anyway?

The Egolian is relishing the despondent nature of the boy. No Orb, no controller, no desire to talk to his friends, no poop. This Hero is most likely gonna end up a zero.

No stress for the Egolian to have to contend with.

Mediocrity is such a safe place to remain, nothing ever happens there.

The school day progresses without too many blips.

Registration went smoothly even with the sarky comment from Mr Winterbottom.

"Blah Blah...... blahhhh blah......
I don't want any drama lamas today.
Blah...... blah.... Blaaaaah."

English, Maths, break time, PE, they all just merged into one big pointless blur to Vinnie.

Completely lost in his thoughts and not paying too much to any attention to his school friends.

Even at lunchtime Vinnie is not his usual self.

"Blimey Vin, you alright? You been well quiet.
I mean, you didn't even laugh when
Tamara accidentally farted in PE.
Squeeeeak it sounded like a strangled duck!! "

Looking around him, Vinnie realises that it is just him and Alfie.

They are standing near the games shed. Everyone else is preoccupied with enjoying their lunchtime to pay too much attention to them.

Vinnie uses this opportunity to confide in his friend.

"Alf, I am worried about my mum and dad.
They have been acting strange, sneaking about,
whispering. And not in a good way.
They are doing that parent thing where they
pretend everything is normal."

He stares at Alfie, taking a breath as he does.

Instantly feeling better to have shared the thoughts and not have them
whirling around and around in his mind.

Alfie ponders the information for a brief moment before turning to Vinnie.

"Mate, that sounds bad.
My mum and dad did that for a bit too,
just before they decided to get a divorce.
And we had to move away...."

Alfie continues to speak to Vinnie, but his voice and the sound of the
playground seems to fall away as the magnitude of what Alfie has said hits
Vinnies's brain.

D... I.. V... O... R... C... E..

Alfie carries on regaling Vinnie with his life story, oblivious to the fear that is being twirled around inside Vinnie by the Egolian at this latest revelation.

"......and as if that is not bad enough – mum now has a boyfriend.."

That last comment pulls Vinnie out of his thoughts and back into the playground.
This is news to him.

"....A boyfriend???..."

He looks at Alfie hoping this last bit was a joke, but Alfie continues.

"Yep. His name is Dave. I hate him. He is such a twonk.
Me and my sister refer to him as 'Dave the Donut'.
Mum moved him in.
Now he struts about like he owns the place."

At that moment, the bell to signal the end of lunchtime goes and all the kids have to line up.

Moved in ??

Vinnies's stomach is now so knotted he feels like he may throw up the tuna sandwich and yogurt tube he ate for lunch.

He can almost feel the partly digested packed lunch pushing its way back up his throat.

He swallows hard as he trudges slowly back to class.

That afternoon's lessons seem to swirl around Vinnie like a fog.
He feels disconnected from the world around him as he focuses on just getting to the end of the day so he can go home and check his dad is still there.

After what felt like an eternity to Vinnie, the teacher signals the end of the day.

The weekend is finally here.

The children leave the classroom with a jubilance only felt on a Friday. The prospect of staying home to do whatever they want for two whole days stretches out in front of the children as they spill from the school gates saying goodbye to their friends as they do.

Normally Vinnie would feel like he was walking on air, but not today. Today his legs feel heavy like he is wearing a pair of boots made of rock.

He can feel the anxiety in his chest as he turns into his road and sees his house up ahead.

Within Vinne, the Egolian is mixing up fears about dad leaving, with the frustration of no Edgebox for a weekend.

They swirl around like an emotional cocktail inside Vinnie.

...Divorce......Dad gone..... moving away...... stuck all weekend with no Edgebox........ bogey brain Ben on my case........

As Vinnie approaches the front door, it opens, and his dad is there to greet him. The immense relief that Vinnie feels as he sees him there propels him forward and he gives him a massive hug.

"Alright, Vin....? This is a nice hello..... How was your day...?"

The normalness of his dad's question and the cheerful surprised tones in his voice cause Vinnie to stop momentarily.

Did I imagine it? Maybe it is me....

Vinnies's thoughts are interrupted by his dad.

"Earth to Vinnie!!
Why don't you go and get out of those school clothes?
Put them in the basket, not your floor!!"

His dad steers him towards the stairs as he speaks, and without saying a word, Vinnie bounds up them to take off the school uniform and get into the weekend vibe.

As he walks into his room, he can feel 'energy'.

An energy that was missing this morning, an energy that Vinnie had missed all day.

"Hero! You are home! How wonderful!"

The Orb seems to appear from nowhere causing Vinnie to jump.

"ORB!! You are here. I thought you had gone forever."

Vinnie can't believe how pleased he feels that The Orb had not gone away and left him.

The Egolian not so much.

It squeezes out some worrying feelings of being abandoned.

"I was always here — you just decided not to see me this morning."

The Orb's explanation does nothing to help Vinnie understand the situation.

"What do you mean?
I *decided* not to see you.
You were definitely not here I would have noticed.
I found the information in the book you left —
that Sean Swarmer fella and his story,
and that random grateful thing you wrote in the book too."

Vinnie's explanation does nothing to help The Orb understand the situation.

"Random grateful thing?

I can assure you, Hero, I wrote nothing in your notebook.

How odd!

Anyway, I was here all along.

You were just unable to see me through the cloud of low energy emotions filling your body.

If you had decided on a different higher energy emotion to feel you would have certainly seen me."

Vinnie stares blankly at The Orb before speaking.

"There you go again, talking about energy and emotions, as if I have any power over them.
It's not me that makes me feel that way. It's all the other annoying people around me who make me feel like that."

The Orb floats near the confused boy.

"Hero, remember how you gave your Egolian the name Brenda?

Remember how that made you feel separate from the Egolian, so that you could see it rather than be it?

That same stratergy can be used with your emotions too.

Once you have identified the emotion, you can find out where in your body it is, and make space for it rather than resist it or let it take control.

Let me show you."

With that, The Orb once again transforms itself into a pair of headphones and attaches itself to Vinnie's confused bonce.

Vinnie closes his eyes and follows the instructions, his chest rising as he inhales a full belly breath and empties it smoothly and slowly.

The Orb detaches itself from Vinnie's head and gives the boy time to process what just transpired.

"I could see my emotions Orby. Like they were little me's inside me. Angry Alan and Desperate Dave were there. I also saw a Silly Simon and Kickbutt Keith. It's like I am made up of lots of Me's. I kinda like that. I have my own little team to help me out. Never thougth of it like that before."

The Orb is impressed at how quickly the Hero is grasping these powerful ideas.

"Well done indeed Hero!
You are well on your way to mastering not only your Egolian but also conquering any fears you may encounter along your way."

Vinnie is loving the praise being heaped upon him, it has brightened his mood and filled him with positivity.

The me's within him do a little victory dance.

The Orb interrupts Vinnie's thoughts with more words of wisdom.

"Hero, well done indeed! By making 'friends' with your emotions you can
work with them rather than fight them or be consumed by them.

You will see the benefits of this new found skill in no time at all.

I have another amazing tool to share with you.
It will build upon this new found recognition of emotions as separate to you.

There are hidden messages you can take from every single
emotion to help steer your path to your true self.

You will see that you have the choice in every situation
to face it from a place of fear or a place of love."

Vinnie looks at The Orb as he ponders this new 'Fear/Love' option.

Maaaaate, this thing is a quackpot.......
If it tries to make me hug a tree,
Or that little vegturd of a brother...
I am outta here......

There is a slight awkwardness in the air surrounding the boy and The Orb following this latest revelation.

This is broken with some final advice from the glowing sphere.

"I have a feeling tonight will be most enjoyable for you Hero.

Perhaps I can suggest you watch the movie 'Inside Out', a very entertaining take on the idea that emotions are separate."

With that, Vinnie leaves the room and heads downstairs.

His ecstatic feelings of seeing The Orb again have been replaced with weirdness in his gut. That is either a result of the thought of hugging his brother or a signal it is close to dinner time.

When he entered the kitchen a takeaway dinner of Peri Peri Chicken and chips had just arrived. Vinnie loves how the spicy coating makes his lips tingle.

The tension from the previous day seemingly disappeared just as The Orb had predicted.

"Let's watch 'Inside Out..'"

If Vinnie had his controller he would have gone straight up to his room after dinner and stayed there the whole evening playing Edgebox with his friends.

He actually couldn't remember the last time they all watched a movie together.

Vinnie sat next to his dad, laughing at the same parts, a feeling of togetherness washing over Vinnie. The twinkle in his dad's eyes as they caught each other's gaze caused Vinnie to forget all about the ghastly week he had experienced.

Ben was sat on the other sofa with mum, they too were enjoying the togetherness of the situation.

The end of the movie signals bedtime for all.

Ben and Vinnie are yawning as they plod up the stairs and into the bathroom to brush their teeth.

Mum and dad are busying themselves downstairs tidying up and switching off lights.

Vinnie is in his room when he hears footsteps on the landing.

It sounded like only one set of feet. Mums' feet. He dismissed the sound, that can't be right.

I expect dad will come up soon...

Vinnie picks up his notebook and writes within it two things he is grateful for today. Switching off his light he whispers to The Orb.

"Night night Orb....... Am glad you are here.

When I wake up. I will feel energised, and excited for the day ahead......"

Before drifting off into a relaxed slumber.

The floofy cat wanders in looking for somewhere cosy to lay its head.

A large 'blanket shaker' casually emitting from the sleeping boy's relaxed bottom causes the floofy menace to rethink its choice, turn and dart back out of the room.

Well, **Reader**. It is, *at last,* the Week of Ends!! How *fantastic!*

Given the **good vibes** the day has **ended** with I *think* the **fears** and worries

our Hero had **yesterday** are *unfounded.*

I have a *feeling* this family **will** live **happily** ever after!

Just like the *stories* portrayed by **that** *Walt Disney* **fella**.

But **Reader**, a *week of ends?!* I **wonder** what it *will bring.*

My **rhyme** is bubbling up ......

The week of ends is here at last,
But let's not forget the recent past.
A torrid time our Hero had,
The school has labelled him as bad.

Bad he is not, just in a bit of a lather,
For he is worried about his father.
What if Alfie is right? what did he say?
Divorce and moving far away?

The day felt like a muted fog,
It dragged along like a two-legged dog.
No happy Friday smiles were to be found,
As our Hero walked homeward bound.

Dad was home when he arrived,
It was a very welcome surprise.
The Orb showed emotions to be,
Like a tiny team of helpful me's.

Take away for dinner they all had,
Then movie time, sat next to dad.
It made them smile and laugh together.
Family time is a time to treasure.

It's like the previous days events were gone,
The family set off for bed with a sleepy yawn.
But our Hero noticed something wrong,
Only one set of footsteps came along.

Drifting to slumber his sleepy head goes,
Grateful things were written before he did doze.
I wonder what tomorrow will bring,
For The Orb will share a 'powerful' thing.

Emotions

Low energy emotions can 'cloud your vision.'

Negative focus

Everything is so awful.

Amazing World

Give your emotion a name:

Sad Sid

Angry Alan

Worried Wayne

Find the <u>emotion</u> in your body,
it will <u>feel</u> like a tense or tight
<u>sensation.</u>

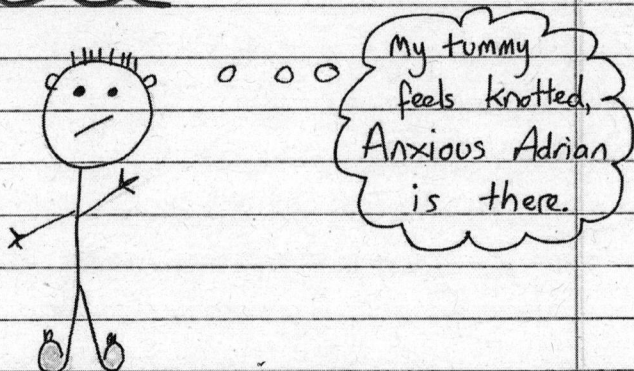

My tummy
feels knotted,
Anxious Adrian
is there.

<u>Be</u> with the emotion, <u>don't try</u>
to <u>fight</u> it or <u>allow it to take</u>
<u>over.</u> <u>Treat it</u> like a friend.

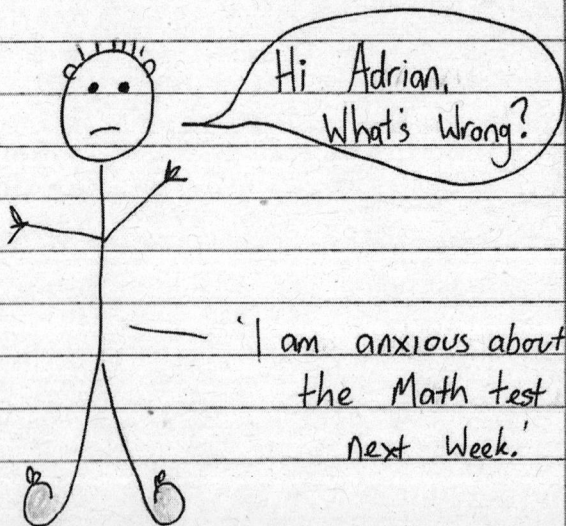

Hi Adrian,
What's Wrong?

'I am anxious about
the Math test
next week.'

I am grateful The Orb is here.

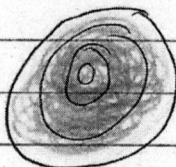
Orby McOrbface

Me

I am grateful I have Alfie to talk to when I am feeling sad.

Me   Alfie

Watch this!

Saturday.

'The failures are the people who never get off their bums.'
Michael Edwards – aka Eddie the Eagle

Good morning **dear Reader.**

The **hour** is **later** *than usual.*

Most of the **family** are *still* sleeping.

A calmness **fills** the *air.*

I am already **enjoying** this 'week of ends' business **very** much.

Even the **floofy cat** of **destruction** is still sleeping *soundly* in its hammock for it is

much tired from its **nighttime** shenanigans, for it went **mouse hunting.**

Quite successfully, I might add **Reader.**

It caught a rather **large** mouse, bought it into the **kitchen** and then promptly

lost it. I *believe* it to be at *this* very moment, **hiding** behind the *refrigerator.*

Yesterday evening seemed to **go** well *for* **all** I would *say,* well everyone, *except*

the poor **mouse.**

That 'Inside Out' movie was most enjoyable. I particularly liked the way at the end where we could see that, although the external elements of Riley's life remained the same – new house, new school, dad being busy with his new venture and such like, it was only when she recognised, listened to and addressed the feelings and emotions within her, she was able to find ways to improve her outlook. This then enabled her to see the positivity all around.

Instead of focusing on the negative.

Just what The Orb has been explaining to our Hero all this week.

Reader, did you also notice that due to these new experiences occurring in Riley's life, her personality islands also increased? This demonstrates how external elements in life, even those perceived as 'bad', can affect internal workings and help cultivate positive attributes like resilience and inner strength.

It's quite marvellous.

Talking of **movies,** did you **see** *that* **Mo Farah** *fella?*

It **can't** have *been* **easy** trying to fit in *with* a **whole** *different* way of **living.**

Coming from **Somalia** *to* **England.** The challenges he had to *face,* and **he** *could*

not speak a **word** of English.

Can **you** *imagine* **Reader,** being in a school *without* understanding a **word** the

people **around** are saying to you? **Must** be a *very* frightening **experience.**

I could *understand* the language **when** we *visited* our **Heros** school, and the **noise**

could be quite deafening at **times. Imagine** that *level of noise* with a language

you **cannot** understand?

It *makes* **me** shudder just *thinking about it.*

I also checked **Mo** out on the *net of inters* and he has a twin brother. When Mo's

family moved to **England,** his *brother* was not well so he stayed in Somalia for a

bit.

When his parents **tried** to *go back* and *get him,* they **couldn't** because a **civil**

war had *broken out.*

Mo ended up **not being** able to **see** his brother for **13 years.**

13 years! I expect our **Hero** would **miss** and *worry* about his brother if **he** was *faced* with this *same* situation.

Despite the **stresses** of the move and the **worries** about members of his family now in **war-torn** Somalia, **Mo** *did not* allow those external factors to affect his **internal desire** to be the **best** he could **be**.

It would have *been* **easy** to have just **given up** and *drifted* through his **life** *feeling* like a **victim** of *circumstance*.

Instead, **Mo** *listened* to his inner **desire,** his **drive** and **smashed it!**

I *wonder* what **words** of **wisdom** The Orb will have for **our** Hero *today*.

It *mentioned* **something** about an amazing **tool** to do *with* **love** and **fear.**

I can feel in *my* water **Reader,** *today* is going to **be most** interesting.

Oh *my* **Reader,** what is that *glorious* smell about the air? It *appears* to be *coming* from the **kitchen.**

What **gloriousness** is this *scent?*

Bay-con? **Reader** *what* is a *Bay-con* for it has stirred a **longing** *deep* within

myself....

Hmmmm *Bayyyy-con*......

Reader *stand* back, let **us** *not venture* past the **staircase** for I *hear* some

footsteps fast **approaching**....

Vinnie is up and walking purposefully along the hallway, as he does the
other members of the household wander from their rooms. Walking silently
down the stairs in a zombie-like trance, they enter the kitchen. No visits to
the loo, no chatting along the way it is as though the family are being drawn
to the kitchen by an invisible force.

Vinnie, dad and Ben enter the kitchen just as bacon sandwiches are being
dished up.

"Good morning my handsome fellas!"

Mum has been for an early run which always leaves her feeling super
energised, at least until 11 am when she will most likely be napping on the
sofa with the floofy cat.

"Hmmmm something smells good...."

"Morning Mum."

"Morning mummy."

Silence descends as mum joins them at the table and the bacon sandwiches are enjoyed. The cat of extraordinary floof is loitering under the table hoping for a morsel of bacon to be dropped.

Vinnie tugs at a small section of bacon rind, it pings out of the sandwich, making his fingers greasy. He quickly pops it under the table for the floofy menace to enjoy.

A roll of the eyes from Mum alerts Vinnie that she has spotted him flouting the 'Don't feed the cat at the table' rule.

He shrugs it off, wipes his greasy hands on his PJ's and continues to enjoy his sandwich.

The heat of the bacon has melted causing it to become a wonderfully warm, gooey delicious mess mixed with the ketchup.

"Looks like its going to be a decent day weather wise, shall we take a walk in the park later?"

Everyone around the table is thrilled with this prospect, except Vinnie. He finds walking boring, too much like hard work.

Vinnie would much rather be running around a large virtual island picking off his opponents and being declared the winner. It feels like an absolute age since he was last playing 'Twice Weekly' with his friends.
Vinnie ponders the situation for a moment.

He looks over at mum.

"Mum, you said I could have my controller back today, remember, you said..."

A sudden silence descends, even the noise of the birds outside seems to have momentarily ceased. There is electricity in the air as mums response is anticipated.

"Vin, you cannot be serious? After the rollercoaster week you
Have had?? I think we can safely say that the Edgebox
will be out of bounds for at least another week."

The air in the kitchen is now so thick with tension it could be cut with a knife.

The occupants of the kitchen wait tentatively for Vinnie's response.

"Ooooooh ma gawwwwwd. Can't believe you just said that!
That's soooooo unfairrrrrrrrr."

With that Vinnie stands up and walks out of the kitchen, slamming the door behind him.

Mums voice can be heard calling after him as Vinnie stomps up the stairs.

"you've got an hour. Then we are all going out......."

Vinnie walks through his bedroom door, slamming it behind him as he does.

"Hero – I heard the commotion from the kitchen.

I think that now is a good time to show you this new tool.

– you will find it most useful."

Vinnie just glares at The Orb.

A familiar feeling in Vinnie's stomach saves The Orb from being hoofed out the bedroom window. Vinnie leaves the room, with a cloud of pre-poop fart behind him.

A not so short while later, Vinnie is back.

His mood has lifted slightly, it's as though the gloriously large poop he just had has taken with it some of the ill-feeling he had been harbouring from the breakfast discussion.

Vinnie busies himself getting dressed for the day. Comfy clothes are the uniform of a Saturday, jogging bottoms and a slogan t-shirt. He chucks his Pj's under his pillow and sets about absentmindedly making his bed.

The Orb watches proudly from across the room.

"Hero, I must say this is a treat to behold.

The bedmaking will continue to put your day on the right track.

Let me show you how to make it more so.."

Vinnie plonks his bottom on the made bed letting out a sigh as he turns to The Orb.

"Go on then....... Tell me what this amazing tool is,
and it better not involve hugging brothers..."

The Orb settles on the bed close to Vinnie and explains.

"This tool is something which has been spoken about and written about for thousands of years.

Even though it is not a new concept, it is still widely ignored by the world we live in.

If more people adopted the concept in their own lives it would positively affect their human experience and that of those around them.

Think of the tool as a type of Emotional Power Pack."

The Orb pauses and looks over at Vinnie who has been momentarily distracted by his fingernail.

The 'Energy Power Pack' statement triggers a glimmer of interest from Vinnie who immediately turns his attention back to The Orb.

An Emotional Power Pack?
That sounds like something from one of my Edgebox games."

The Orb shines brightly, realising that the concept of power and energy may not be such a new thing for the Hero after all.

"Indeed it is Hero!

Take hold of your notebook for I have placed something helpful within it."

Vinnie picks up his notebook and opens it on the next available page. Within it is the image of a sort of battery. There are words written inside it. As he stares at it, reading the words The Orb explains.

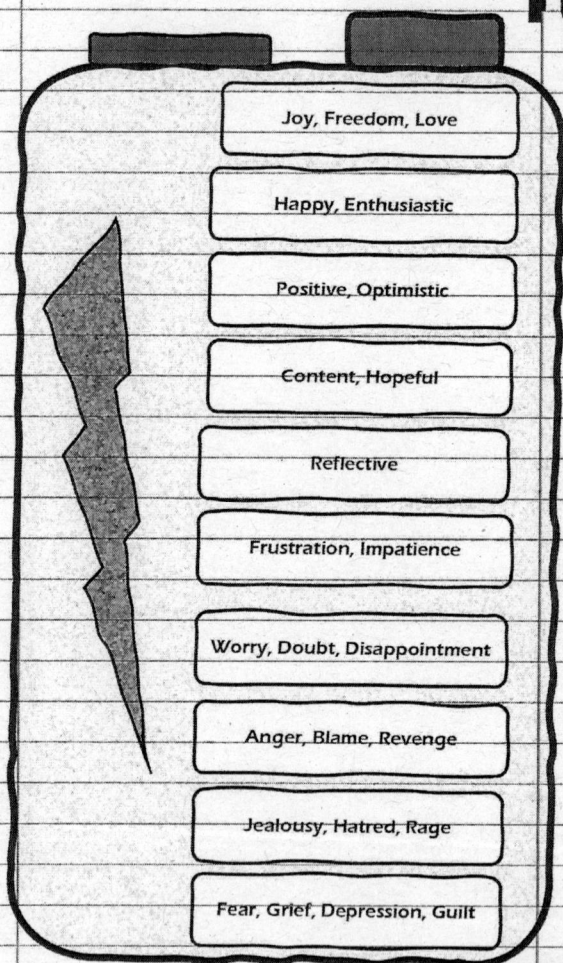

Emotional Powerpack *

FULL

- Joy, Freedom, Love
- Happy, Enthusiastic
- Positive, Optimistic
- Content, Hopeful
- Reflective
- Frustration, Impatience
- Worry, Doubt, Disappointment
- Anger, Blame, Revenge
- Jealousy, Hatred, Rage
- Fear, Grief, Depression, Guilt

EMPTY

*Emotional Power Pack and its use is adapted from: Esther Hicks Emotional Guidance Scale & Sir David Hawkins Letting Go technique.

"This is a powerful tool as it will help you to understand the power behind the emotions that you feel.

Each emotion is sending you a message.
Emotions are not what rule you.

That is where many people can get it wrong.

When they feel an emotion,
they allow themselves to be swept along by the feeling.

But emotions require deciphering."

The Orb pauses briefly to allow Vinnie to take in what it has just declared.

"Deciphering? Isn't that what you do with a code?
We learnt about that word at school..
But emotions are not a code Orby.
I think you may be a bit wrong there..."

The Orb moves closer to Vinnie so that it is hovering just above the bed next to him.

"Ok. This is an unusual concept to understand.

Even many adults have no idea that their emotions are a tool to help them as they blindly stumble through life making the same mistakes over and over again.

Giving their power away instead of harnessing it and using it to propel them to greatness beyond their wildest dreams....."

The Orb had completely forgotten itself for a moment as it launched into another well-meaning motivational speech.

It turns its attention back to Vinnie.

"Ok Hero.
Let's think of it as an energy source.

You recognised it as being similar to that used within the Edgebox games.

When the characters' power runs low you must find something that boosts it."

Vinnie's eyes light up as he recalls the games. This is something he can get a grip with, he is ace at finding hidden sources of power within the games.

He listens attentively as The Orb continues.

"At the end are low vibrational emotions.
You remember how we spoke,
about the Universe being made up of energy and vibrations?"

Vinnie nods and smiles.

He is eager to hear how this all links to the power pack.
This life business may be more like a game than he had realised.

The Orb continues.

"Let's refer back to your school day the other day, you know,
the one where you got sent to the headteachers office. Which day was that?"

"Thursday, that day was Thursday."

Vinnie responds with some trepidation. That was not his favourite day of the week, not one he wants to dwell on for too long.

"Thursday, yes, yes.
That was the one.
Think back to the moment where it all went wrong.

When was that?"

Vinnie pauses for a moment as he thinks back to Thursday.

"Well, everything was OK.
Until Mr Winterbutthole called me an idiot."

The memory of that moment casts a shadow over Vinnie's face and a twisty feeling in the pit of his stomach.

Brenda enjoyed that day very much and is now relishing the emergence of the memories flooding back and filling this so-called Hero with negativity.

"So Hero, now look at the Emotional Powerpack.
What emotion were you feeling when Mr Winterbottom
used the word 'idiot'?"

Vinnie looks at the power bank and it takes him no time to select the emotion he was feeling on that fateful Thursday.

"Rage! I would say.
It was much stronger than anger.
I felt it building up inside of me,
and then it just went a bit mental."

The Egolian cannot believe The Orb is being so stupid. How on earth can it think that this will help? The manifestation of low vibrational emotions are now coursing through the boy.

After a short pause, The Orb speaks again.

"Let's take a moment to really think back now to Thursday.

Was Mr Winterbottom using the term idiot the real reason you got so raged?"

Vinnie looks at The Orb, he is not sure where this line of questioning is going but is quite sure The Orb may be the 'blithering idiot'.

Vinnie sighs as he responds.

"Well, of course, it was Orb.
He called me a 'blithering idiot' in front of the
whole class and they laughed at me."

The Orb starts to change into the headphones once again.

Vinnie sees it coming towards him and ducks to avoid it. He is not in the mood for sniffing farts or monkey chatter.

The Orb swings around the back of Vinnie and secures itself to the boys head before he has a chance to getaway.

A calmness enters the room.

The Egolian wishes the blasted Orb would stop doing that.

It is proper messing up its comfort zone plans.

As The Orb returns to its normal shape, it turns to Vinnie.

"Hero, I could feel the Egolian inside you feeding those feelings of rage and unfairness within you.

It was trying to blind you to the truth about what happened on Thursday.

The mediation we just did is something you can use whenever you feel like you need to gently re-set to allow you to be more present in the now.

You were in danger of being stuck in the emotional state of rage you felt on Thursday and that would have affected the rest of your day and possibly your whole weekend.

            And not in a good way!"

Vinnie smiles fondly at The Orb, he does indeed feel more present, more aware of his surroundings and more able to reflect on the past without it affecting his present.

The Egolian is in a state of constipated shock at the power of this mediation malarky.

It is powerless against it.

The Orb speaks again to the boy.

"So, let's think back to Thursday.
What were you really feeling?"

Vinnie looks again at the emotional power pack, a brief pause ensues before he turns back to The Orb.

"Well. I guess I was feeling worried. I am worried about my mum and dad. I think something is going on that they are not telling me about.".

The Orb presses Vinnie further.

"Looking at the power pack again,
how does it make you feel
when you think they are hiding something from you?"

Turning his attention to the power pack once more, Vinnie responds.

"I feel angry... no, that is not right.
Frustrated, I feel frustrated that they think I'm too stupid to notice.

I just want them to answer me truthfully when I ask them if everything is alright."

The Orb is impressed that Vinnie recognised that frustration was the dominant emotion at that time, it wasn't anger at all.

"Excellent awareness Hero, you will see that the next level is 'reflective'.

This is now your current state.

As we reflect on where we are now.

Look again at the power pack.

Use it to lift your positive energy further.

Talk me through it.

Remember that this needs to be coming from within.

What can you do?"

Vinnie once again turns his attention to the power pack, this time he ponders the remaining bars.

"Okay. I think I get this now. So, up until this point I have been worried about my mum and dad.

It frustrates me because they try to hide stuff from me.

They treat me like I'm an idiot..."

Vinnie suddenly stops talking.

A moment of clarity has just occurred, like a lightbulb turned on in his mind.

In stunned disbelief, he turns back to The Orb.

"Orby. I don't think I was cross
with Mr Winterbottom at all.
I was cross with my mum and dad."

A silence has descended upon the room. Vinnie is sitting very still, this understanding of the emotional turmoil he was feeling on that Thursday has bought with it feelings of wonder, calmness, and curiosity.

The Orb floats near, its warm glow reflecting the calmness emanating from Vinnie.

"And, another thing Hero.

If you think carefully about what Mr Winterbottom actually said.

You will find that he said you are NOT a blithering idiot.

You were so disconnected from the now, so caught up in the past events from that morning, so worried and frustrated, that you heard what you were tuned in to hear.

Your perspective was altered by what was going on inside you and you projected that out to Mr Winterbottom."

The room is once again bathed in silence as The Orb allows Vinnie to contemplate this new insight into what actually happened that Thursday.

I feel mum and dad treat me like an actual idiot....

It sounded at the time like Mr Winterbottom called me an actual idiot....

The Orb moves closer to Vinnie for it knows that this next piece of information may be difficult to hear.

"One other thing Hero,

Mr Winterbottom was not actually angry with you at all.

He was having his own internal struggle.

He had to have his pet dog of fourteen years put to sleep at the vets Wednesday evening. The dog had been quite poorly for a while and it was a very difficult decision for Mr Winterbottom to make.

He was feeling a mixture of grief for his loss and also huge guilt for having had to make that most painful of decisions."

Once again a silence descends.

I'd hate to have to do that with the cat

I really love that ball of fluff....

Vinnie is lost in thought as he thinks about Mr Winterbottom and his dog.

The Orb motions for Vinnie to turn his attention once again to the Emotional Power Pack.

"Do you see how the emotional power pack allows you to investigate the
meanings behind the emotion?
The more you use this skill,
the more easily it will come to you during situations.
Using it to reflect upon situations builds upon this amazing skill which will
allow you to find the path to your truest self.
Let's look at the next power-up."

Vinnie turns back to the power pack.

"Next one up... I would choose 'Hopeful'.
I am hoping my mum and dad are ok and that they stop trying to hide stuff from me. I am hoping to get a new Edgebox controller soon......... Next, I would probably go with 'Optimistic'. I am optimistic that they will find a way to sort everything out and we won't have to move and I will absolutely get a new Edgebox controller."

There is a short pause, as the feelings of optimism do indeed course through Vinnie's body. He smiles to himself as he looks at the Power Pack.

The Egolian inside him is struggling. It can feel itself being twisted and rung out. Like a wet towel.

This power pack needs to be lost.

The energy emanating from the boy right now is stifling any ability it has to project feelings of fear and doubt.

"Now I choose 'Happy'.
I am happy that my tummy no longer feels sick.

Next is 'Free'! I feel free!
It is the weekend and I have no school!"

With that, a very triumphant Vinnie sits up,
and looks at The Orb.

The Orb is feeling equally jubilant at the current state of events.

"Hurrah Hero!

You did it! You have not changed anything about the external situation.
But, you have altered your internal state of being.
You are positively glowing with positivity!
Now with this positivity flowing through you,
What can you do to help your present situation?
You cannot make people do things they don't want to,
But you can control how they behave towards you.

If you want people to be kind and patient with you, then you must first be
kind and patient with yourself and others.

People will mirror the characteristics back to you.

You will attract people and situations which are a vibrational match.

If you are vibrating at the lower end of the Power Pack you will not only feel
drained but you will also create more of the same around you.

So always act from a place of love rather than hate."

Vinnie does indeed feel amazing inside having worked his way up the Power Pack. He feels like he could handle anything right about now. He contemplates other elements of The Orbs recent teachings.

> Come to think of it, making the bed does make me feel good. And it made mum be nice to me about the Edgebox controller.
>
> The sentence also makes me feel good as I drift off to sleep.
>
> Maybe The Orb has a point....

One thing is puzzling Vinnie as he turns his attention back to The Orb.

> "So, how do you know about Mr Winterbottom's dog? I know he hasn't told anyone otherwise the whole school would have been talking about it..."

There is a brief pause before The Orb responds.

It hadn't expected to share this level of information so soon.

"I heard about it from Mr Winterbottom's Essence Orb."

This last sentence catches Vinnie completely off guard.

"Mr Winterbottom has an Essence Orb too?
Is there some sort of Orby club that you
all meet up in??"

Settling next to Vinnie, The Orb explains.

"Everyone on the planet has an Essence Orb.
Some are lost in their comfort zone, others are at various stages of Hero development.

All are linked to each other.

Mr Winterbottom's is a fully-fledged Hero Orb."

Vinnie stares at The Orb in continued disbelief.

"All Orbs are connected?
     What does that mean?
        Mr Winterbottom a Hero, are you sure??"

The Orb glows as it continues with its explanation.

"Yes Hero, it is true.
All Essence Orbs are connected, what affects one Orb affects all Orbs.
Mr Winterbottom dreamed of being a teacher when he was very little.
It is all he has ever wanted to be.
He followed his heart, did what was necessary to make his dream come true,
                        and is now living his true purpose."

The Orb pauses to allow Vinnie's brain time to digest this avalanche of information, before continuing.

Mr Winterbottom a Hero!

Who'd have guessed it?

"Do not forget Hero, that Mr Winterbottom is a person with emotions just like you.

He is in his first year of teaching and is nervous about making a mistake, he has feelings of not being good enough.

Even though he followed his heart, his head can be full of doubts."

The Orb is suddenly interrupted by mum shouting up the stairs.

"Vinnie, get ready.

   We are leaving for the park in 10 minutes."

Vinnie groans, as he turns to The Orb.

"Ah, maaaan. I had hope that idea would have been forgotten."

Vinnie finds his trainers and laces them up as The Orb speaks.

"Hero, use this walk as an opportunity to be completely in the now.

Breathe in the fresh air and really look around you at the wonder of the natural world.

Open your mind, you may actually enjoy this experience.

Oh, and one last thing, maybe another family movie night is in order.

I would suggest watching the 'Eddie the Eagle' story."

Vinnie opens the bedroom door to join his family, who can be heard getting their coats on at the bottom of the stairs.

"Maybe, but I am not very interested in eagles."

The Orb chuckles to itself as it responds.

"Well, this is not your average eagle."

Vinnie shrugs as he leaves the room to join his family.
The walk in the park was different for Vinnie than usual.

Usually, he just saw it as an unnecessary interruption to his Edgebox
gaming, with his mind full of Edgebox gaming and his body full of
resentment.

But today he felt a freedom that he had never really encountered before. He
looked about him as they walked through the park. He could see the leaves
on the trees, the flowers littering the ground and he noticed the soft breeze
on his face as he walked.

He could hear the gentle snap of twigs beneath his feet as he walked along.
At one point Ben stepped in a large pile of poop. The dog that dropped that
must have been the size of a T-Rex.

Ordinarily, Vinnie would have laughed at Ben's misfortune. He would
probably have invented a new hilarious name for him like 'Poo foot Ben', and
ran away from him every time he came close.

But not today. Today Vinnie looked at Ben's misfortune and thought about
how he would feel if it had happened to him. If it was him, he would like to
get it off his shoe as quickly as possible before the smell made him vomit.

Looking around, Vinnie realised that mum and dad had dropped behind and
it would be a few minutes before they caught up to them.

So, Vinnie showed Ben to a patch of grass and demonstrated how to remove
the poo by aggressively rubbing his foot along it.

By the time mum and dad had caught up, the poo incident had been taken
care of and Ben was beaming at his big brother as though he was an actual
superhero.

After the walk and a quick go on the swings at the children's park, Dad
suggested pizza for lunch. Not just any pizza, this was pizza at a place
where you played ping pong too!

A few games were played, Vinnie had his favourite BBQ chicken pizza whilst Ben had a Hawaiian. Vinnie will never understand fruit on a pizza.

That evening they watched the movie recommended by Vinnie. The family all agreed, after all, Vinnie's recent movie requests had all been spot on.

This one was no different.

Vinnie went to bed that night feeling safe and optimistic.

"When I wake up, I will feel
Energised and excited for the day ahead."

Oh, **Reader** of the words *rejoice!*

Our **Hero's** journey must *surely* **be** much improved with the **addition** of a

Power Pack!

I cannot **wait** to *see* the next **instalment** of this *exciting* **journey** called life!

Rhyme **time!!**

An amazing smell filled the air,
bacon sandwiches for all to share.
No controller, he is told by mum,
this threatens to ruin our Hero's fun.

Back in his room, with a door slammed,
The Orb has a tool to help him understand.
Emotions are clues that need deciphering
They help create a life so inspiring.

Low vibrational emotions drain us so,
High vibrational emotions are the way to go!
Use the Power Pack to find your state,
Look to the next level, how can you relate?

This tool will empower all Hero's around
And with it their true purpose found.
Follow your joy, love conquers all.
To wallow in hate turns a Hero into a fool.

Reader, I see the notebook there,
Go see for yourself, where do you fare?
Power up your own emotional pack
To ensure YOUR dreams stay on track.

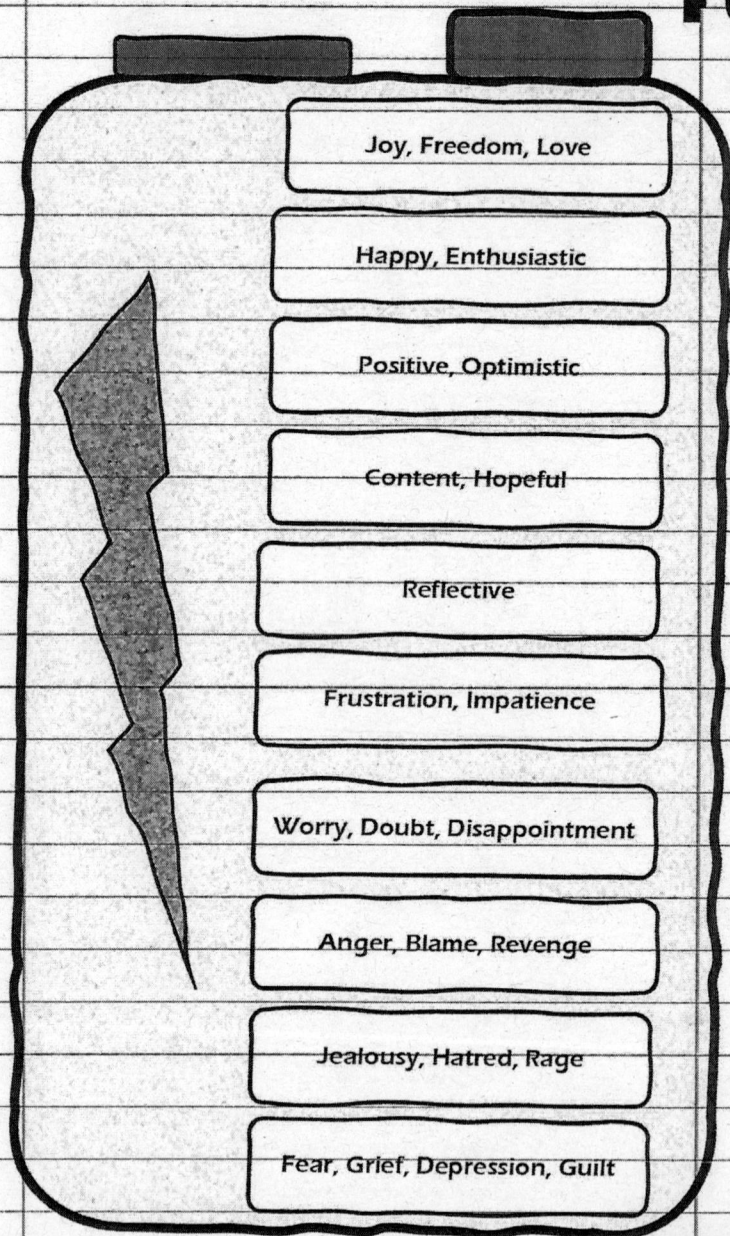

Emotional Powerpack

FULL

Joy, Freedom, Love

Happy, Enthusiastic

Positive, Optimistic

Content, Hopeful

Reflective

Frustration, Impatience

Worry, Doubt, Disappointment

Anger, Blame, Revenge

Jealousy, Hatred, Rage

Fear, Grief, Depression, Guilt

EMPTY

Emotional Power Pack

Can use during a situation or after to reflect upon stuff and how it played out.

1. Find the emotional level.

> I am feeling frustrated...

2. Think about what triggered the emotion.

> I can't get to the next level on my game.

3. What is the next level up?

Next is Reflective, then Content and hopeful...

4. How can you get there?

Well, I can be content that I have got this far already or I can keep trying, never losing hope that I can do it!

5. Check in. How do you feel now? Can you go any higher?

Wowee! Now I feel Super Positive!

Remember YOU are in control and can CHOOSE how you feel.

I can choose to stay frustrated or I can choose content, hopeful or positive!

If you are struggling to regain control from an emotion, get back into 'The Now'.

Close my eyes, breathe in pizza. Visualise the room I am in ...

I am grateful that mum made me a bacon sandwich for breakfast.

I am grateful I was able to help Ben with his poopy shoe.

Watch this....

Sunday.

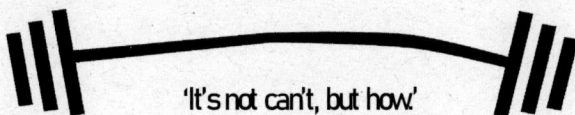

> 'It's not can't, but how.'
> *Nick Santonastasso*

Well good *morning* dear **Reader.**

What a **glorious** thing this *week of ends* is!

I am much *looking* forwards to *seeing* what **tomorrows** *week of ends day* will bring.

Huh!? **Reader**, *surely not!* A *week of ends* is only **two days** long?

What utter **nonsense** is *this?* Tomorrow is **Monday?** *Does that mean* **we** need to *go back* to **s-s-s-school?**

Yes, *yes* I *know.* **Norman** is relishing my sudden **attack of** *nerves*. What *can* I do?

Reader, you are the *wisest* of **humans** I *know.*

Of *course!*   Let's use the **Power Pack** in our Hero's *notebook.*

Hmmmmm, I can *say* that the emotion I *am* registering is that of **worry.**

I *am* **worried** *because* the **school** is *so* loud.

I *do not* like **loud noises**, *they* make **me** *feel* frustrated and *uncomfortable.*

Look, *look,* **Reader,** I *have* moved up, I *am* now on **reflective.** If I look at *my* **internal emotion** now, it is hopeful! *Yes,* I *would say* I *feel* full of hope, in fact, I *can* **go** one *better.* I *am* optimistic that **next** week at *school* will be *much* **better** than *last.*

I *know* the school *will be* **noisy,** that I cannot **change** *but* at least I am *prepared* for it. Let **me** think *back* to the **noisiness.** Why *is it* so **noisy?** Well, there *are* **many,** many **children** and *they* are chatting and *laughing* **together.**

Why **Reader,** when I *think* about it, all *that* **noise** *actually* stems from **happy,** enthusiastic **children.** *My* mind distorted *my* perception of the **situation** and *all* I focused **on** was the **volume,** the unexpectedness of the situation **blinded** me to what I was **witnessing.** I bet that *if* I had taken a *moment* to stay in the **nowness** of the moment, and not *allowed* **myself** to *have been* **distracted** by the fear within, I *would have* noticed **other** *things*. **More** *positive* things, like the **smiles** on the children's **faces** and the *excited* **tones** of *their chatter.*

I *do believe* that tomorrow when **we** *reenter* the **school,** I will feel **joy!** JOY at being *part* of a **wonderful** experience *where* we will learn *new* things and get to *run around* with the other **children** in the *playground.*

Gosh. I *am* quite **looking** *forward* to the return to **school** *now!* What an *amazingly* **simple** but effective tool The **Orb** did share.

I *suspect* that Eddie the Eagle fella hovers around **positive**, **optimistic**. *enthusiastic* and joy. **Never** *giving* up.

He **never** *lost sight* of his dream to be an 'Olympian.' He *didn't* know *how* **he** would *manage* it.
He *focused* on the **end goal**, he imagined **himself** at the Olympic **Games** *over* and *over* **again**.

The **positive** *vibes* this **generated** *allowed* Eddie to **see** opportunities to *bring him closer* to his **dream** and he **grabbed** them without a **moment's** *hesitation!* Eddie would have experienced doubts and worry, *after all,* **he** is human and it *would* be only natural to *feel this,* **but** he *did not allow* **himself** to be distracted *by it.* **He** *did not allow* it to cloud his *vision* or dampen his spirits.

Once again, we *can see* **Reader** that *the strongest* **attribute** of *any* Hero is a *determination to succeed.*

It is worth *remembering* **Reader,** that **Eddie** *did not win* any medals. In fact, he **came last** in *both* the 70m and 90m *ski jumping events.* It was not the medals that made this **Hero** a winner. It was **his** *commitment* and *determination.* **Eddie** was the first Britain to **compete** in the Ski jumping *event* since 1928! **Reader,** that was an astonishing 60 years passing *between* the last **British ski jumping** competitor and *Eddie's entry.*

Eddie the Eagle is a *superstar* **Hero** *because* he **never gave up**, despite people *making* **negative** assumptions *about him.* Initially, Eddie was treated *like a joke* and it would have *been easy* for him to have *turned his back* on his **dream**. **But** he *followed his heart* and is still benefiting from it today, some 33 years later.

Reader, this planet, *this world* is overflowing with **Hero's**.
It *makes me feel* so honoured to *be able* to **witness** the abundance of
Hero's like Eddie *giving it their all* and like Mr Winterbottom *fulfilling*
his *dream to teach*.

I *am feeling* very **warm and fuzzy** inside Reader.
So *warm and fuzzy* that all *feelings of worry* have disappeared.

Oh Reader, *what* wonderful day we have *ahead of us*, I can feel it in **my**
every **fibre**.

The house is *quiet,* there must be **no one awake.** *Not even* the floofy cat *stirs.*

Let us *take a* peek at our Hero and *see* if **his** *dreams* are improved.

Gently through *his* bedroom door, we go Reader.

Ah, *there* he *is.*
A small *smile* sits upon his *peaceful* face.

He *dreams,* Reader, he *does indeed* dream.

In *his* dream, *he is* a **superhero.** His *outfit* is *green and red* with a poop emoji on the *cape*. He *wears* a mask *across* his eyes to *hide his identity* as he *swoops the earth.*

The earth has been taken **over** by dinosaurs. **Huge** *alien* dinosaurs! They wander the earth *destroying* everything in their *path* with their massive, *steaming,* **stinking** poops.

Our *caped* **Hero** must thwart *their* progress *before* they cover the *entire* planet in **putrid** poop.

With the Pooper Hero's *power* of levitation, he is *able* to lift a *steaming* poop off *some* frightened people, **he** *swings* it round in the air and *sends* it *flying* into the face of the dinosaur who dropped **it**.

Wailing, the dinosaur flees *back* to the spaceship from *where* it had emerged and *takes off.*

Look, **Reader**, *see* the smile of *contentment* on our Hero's *sleeping face* is now a smile of victory as he *flies* around the **planet** *flinging* **poop** in *all* the other *dinosaurs* faces. *They* run to *their* space ships with faces **full** of faeces!

The entire *planet* is eternally *grateful* to the **masked crusader** with the *first-class aim.* The dream is *fading.*

Reader, our **Hero** *awakes...*

The sleepy boy turns over and shoves both hands under his pillow, as a large windy popper escapes from his not so sleepy bottom.

The escaping parp causes Vinnie to stir from his superhero slumber and he opens his eyes, in doing so all dreams of pooping dinosaurs disappear without a trace.

Sitting up and yawning, Vinnie looks at the time on his phone. It has only just gone 7.30 am. He is a bit perplexed at being up so early on a Sunday, usually, he would have played his Edgebox until the early hours of the morning, secretly of course for mum and dad make him turn it off at 10.30 pm. Vinnie would have just turned it back on again once they have both gone to bed.

Lying in his cosy bed, arms bent behind his head, he gazes up at the ceiling.

Before long Vinnie's attention is drawn to the faint sound of someone up and about downstairs. Stretching himself full length in bed with arms above his head, he decides to go and see who else is up so early.

He wanders down the stairs, no floofy cat looming in the stairwell as it is still very much asleep, snuggled in the basket of clean laundry sitting at the bottom of the stairs.

It opens one sleepy eye as Vinnie passes.

The gentle noise of someone moving around is coming from the kitchen. Vinnie pushes open the door as mum is busying herself with the kettle.

Lost in thought as Vinnie enters the room she doesn't notice him approach the table where her laptop sits open.

"Morning Mum..."

This unexpected greeting causes her to jump.

**"Blimey Vin, you gave me a fright!
Morning, why are you up so early on a Sunday!"**

Responds mum, as she moves quickly to the open laptop, snapping it shut with one hand whilst steadying the cup of coffee in her other hand.

She sits down at the table,
a forced smile upon her weary face.

Vinnie had managed to catch a look at the open page on the laptop just before mum snapped it shut. He is suddenly feeling quite off-balanced like the walls are closing in. The sounds of the kitchen fall away and all he can hear is the blood rushing in his ears.

"I just um, need the um, loo..."

Stammers Vinnie as he rushes out of the kitchen as quickly as he can. He bounds up the stairs and does indeed rush straight into the loo. His tummy is feeling very strange indeed as his morning poop makes a rushed appearance.

The Egolian inside is mustering up as many worrying vibes as it can. Heading back into his bedroom, Vinnie sits on his bed, bewildered and scared.

"Hero, Whatever is the matter?"

The Orb appears from the top of the wardrobe and settles itself next to the shell shocked boy.

"I have just found mum in the kitchen.
she was looking at flats for rent.
Why would she be looking for somewhere else to live?

Why?

I feel so sick."

A silence descends the room as the worried boy's words echo around.

"Hero, you are experiencing a reaction to worry.

It manifests itself in your body as stress.

Let's take a moment to bring you back to the present moment by becoming aware of your body.

Sit still and feel how the air hugs around your body like a comforting blanket.

Hear your breath, in and out, feel the rise and fall of your chest.

When you breathe deeper, can you pick up any smells?"

The Orb pauses for a moment as it allows Vinnie to feel the air around him, to listen to his breathing and to pick up on any smells present.

Vinnie's mind has drifted from the laptop screen and is, as instructed, contemplating the smells around him.

I don't know how smelling is going to help me. To be fair all I smell is a kinda cheese, why is there cheese in my bedroom?

Oh, I think that smell is my feet.....

The Orb continues.

"Remember Hero,

worry is not all bad.

Worry is there to keep us safe but if we get carried away with the feeling of worry it can drain us.

Think back to the Emotional Power Pack, where did worry feature in the power levels?"

Vinnie ponders the question for a moment. Leaning over to open his notebook back at the Power Pack page.

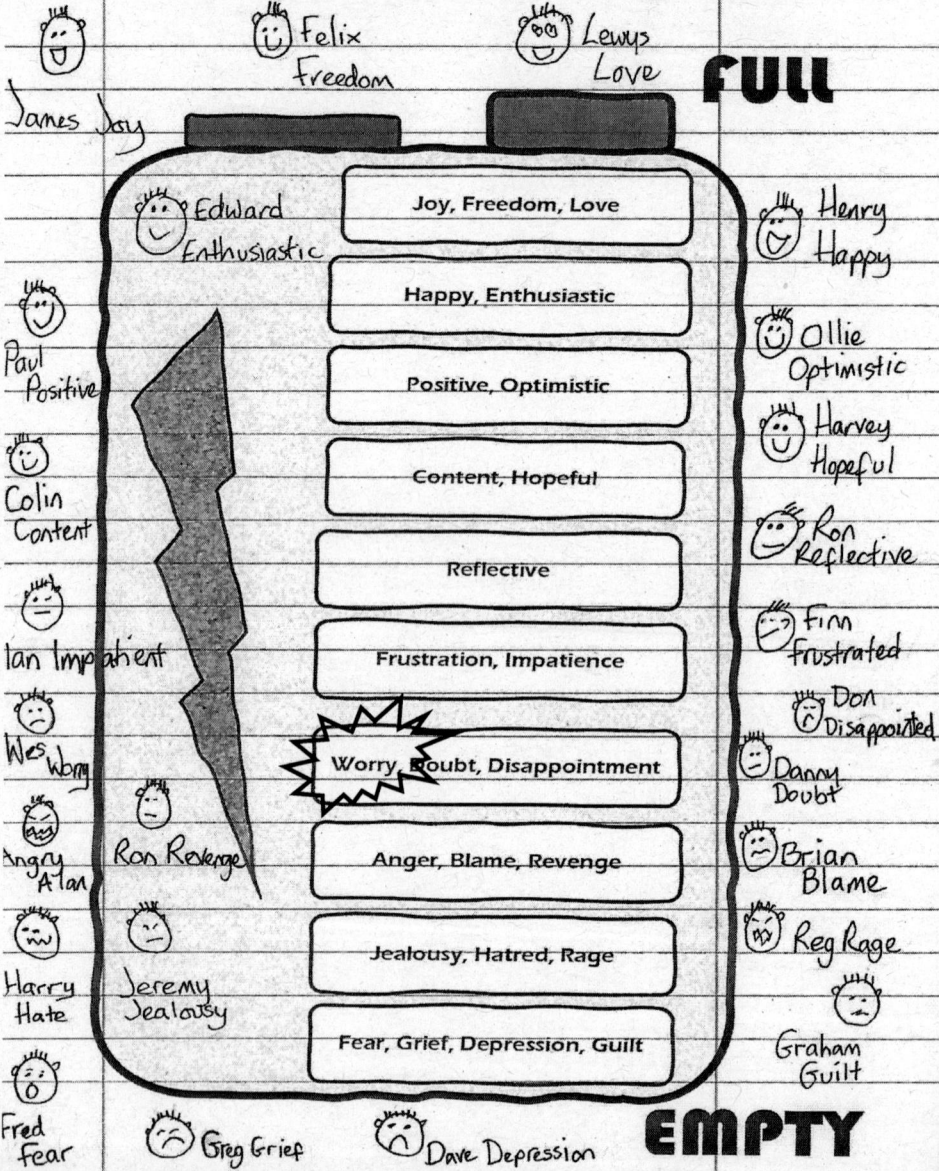

Emotional Powerpack

FULL

James Joy

Felix Freedom

Lewys Love

| Joy, Freedom, Love |

Edward Enthusiastic

Henry Happy

| Happy, Enthusiastic |

Paul Positive

Ollie Optimistic

| Positive, Optimistic |

Colin Content

Harvey Hopeful

| Content, Hopeful |

Ron Reflective

| Reflective |

Ian Impatient

Finn Frustrated

| Frustration, Impatience |

Wes Worry

Don Disappointed

| Worry, Doubt, Disappointment |

Danny Doubt

Angry Alan

Ron Revenge

| Anger, Blame, Revenge |

Brian Blame

Harry Hate

Jeremy Jealousy

| Jealousy, Hatred, Rage |

Reg Rage

| Fear, Grief, Depression, Guilt |

Graham Guilt

Fred Fear

Greg Grief

Dave Depression

EMPTY

Finding it, he turns to the Orb.

"It's quite low down Orby. This means it is a low vibrational energy, right?"

Impressed with the boy's response and understanding the Orb continues.

"Yes, yes indeed Hero!

Well done.

Now you have a choice to use the worry feelings to be a strength or a weakness.

Will you choose to let it drag you and your energy further down or will you gain control over it and turn it into higher vibrational energy?"

Vinnie looks at The Orb, now he is not only worried about the flat hunting but The Orb's last question has added the worry about having low vibrational energy and not knowing what to do about it.

"I thought you were supposed to be helping me. Now I am more worried than ever."

Vinnie sits on the bed, his gaze falls to his hands in his lap. His shoulders are hunched as if they are carrying a great weight.

Brenda is chucking up a great wave of worrying feelings,
mixing a little bit of fear,
and uncertainty into the mix for good measure.

Seeing the poor boy's demeanour, The Orb transforms itself into headphones and nestles on Vinnie's head.

Within no time at all,
 a smile appears on Vinnie's face.

As quickly as it came, it is then replaced by a worried look.

And then a smile.

The smile remained in place this time even after The Orb detaches itself from Vinnie's head. The smile remains, and his previously hunched back and shoulders are now upright, confident and strong.

"Can I really do that myself Orby? When I feel worried? Will I not need you to show me?"

The room has a calm energy about it, tinged with positivity emanating from the newfound power in the tool Vinnie just learned.

The Egolian is close to tears at this new development.

The annoying Orb has just given the boy a superpower.

"Oh yes, Hero!

You will be able to harness the power of that positive thought and its feelings whenever you are in a place of stress.

You could even use it when having to visit the dentist or have an immunisation needle.

Just allow your mind to take you back to that positive place and mindset.

It won't change the external situation but it will change how you deal with it which in turn will create a positively awesome reality."

There is silence in the room now as Vinnie relishes this new feeling of strength that runs through his being.

He is interrupted by The Orb.

"Hero, as well as the positive place mindset you just created, what other things do you know you can use to lift your vibration?

Think about what makes you feel good, what makes you feel alive and happy?"

Vinnie ponders the question, reflecting on the things that make him feel good inside.

"Well, I love the Edgebox games. It makes me feel good to chat with my friends and show off my skills. Those movies you told me about make me feel good, especially Eddie the Eagle and Bethany. Watching them become great gave me a warm fuzzy feeling inside. Oh and that song Happy with all the people dancing gave me a smile and made me want to dance. Going for a walk with mum, dad and even Ben was cool too.

Orby, I do have the power to change my thoughts. I really do have the power to control how I can feel."

This latest revelation of awareness from the boy has given Brenda a most uncomfortable feeling of dread. It can feel itself being pushed to the side by 'Harvey Hopeful' and 'Paul Positive'.

It really hates those guys.......

Sounds from downstairs float into the room, the rest of the house is up and about. Vinnie realises that at least an hour has passed since he saw the laptop and even though nothing has changed since then, he feels different.

Vinnie picks up the Emotional Powerpack to see if he is right.

Emotional Powerpack

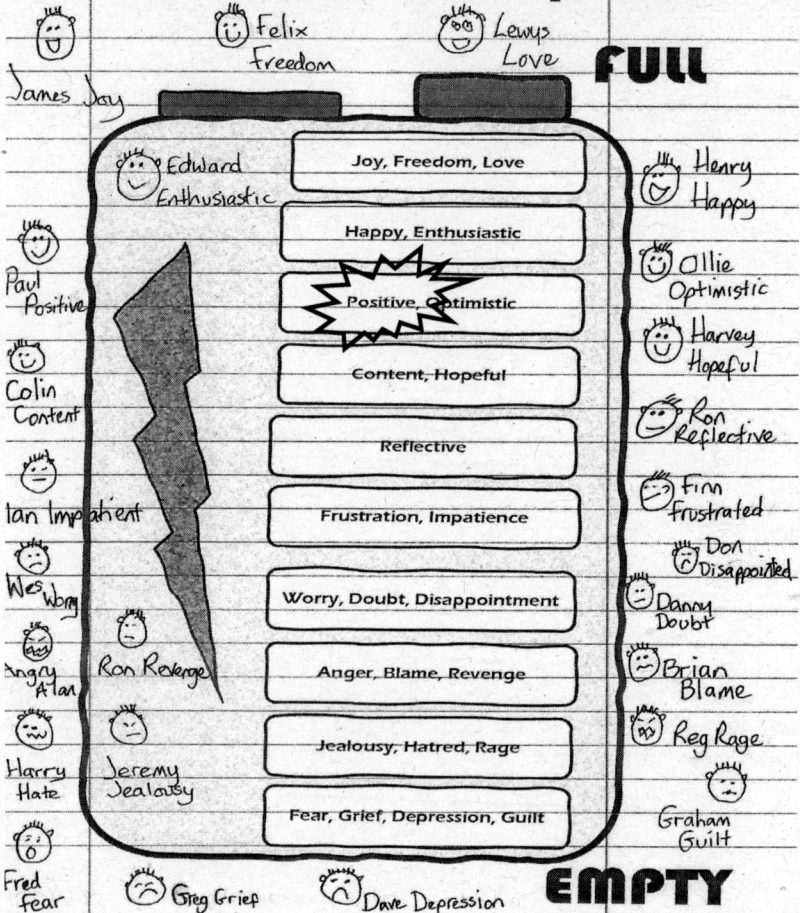

James Joy   Felix Freedom   Lewys Love   **FULL**

Edward Enthusiastic   Henry Happy

Paul Positive   Ollie Optimistic

Colin Content   Harvey Hopeful

Ian Impatient   Ron Reflective

Wes Worry   Finn Frustrated

Angry Alan   Ron Revenge   Don Disappointed

Harry Hate   Jeremy Jealousy   Danny Doubt

Fred Fear   Greg Grief   Dave Depression   Brian Blame   Reg Rage   Graham Guilt   **EMPTY**

- Joy, Freedom, Love
- Happy, Enthusiastic
- Positive, Optimistic
- Content, Hopeful
- Reflective
- Frustration, Impatience
- Worry, Doubt, Disappointment
- Anger, Blame, Revenge
- Jealousy, Hatred, Rage
- Fear, Grief, Depression, Guilt

The feelings of worry have all but gone, they are not gone completely but, they are not consuming his every thought.

Looking at the power pack, Vinnie recognises that if he had not had The Orb teach him this new strategy he would now have feelings of anger and blame in him.

His vibrational energy would have dipped lower and lower.

A smile of satisfaction and empowerment sits on his face,
as he recognises The Orb and its waffle about vibrations,
energy and inner power are very real indeed.

The energy of the room changes at once when a voice calls up the stairs.

"Vin, can you come downstairs please,
we need to talk to you.............."

It is mum.

This type of request is never usually a good thing.

Vinnie stands up and walks towards the door,
the worry feelings are taking hold again.

Taking a deep breath, and feeling the floor beneath his feet to ground
himself in the 'Now', Vinnie leaves the room and ventures downstairs.

The kitchen is a hive of activity when Vinnie enters. Mum is tidying away
breakfast items while Ben shoves the final spoon of cereal into his mouth.
Dad is near the back door tickling the cat on its floofy tummy.

"Gaaaahhhhhhhhhh!!"

Dad lets out a sudden yelp of pain, causing all eyes in the kitchen to turn in his direction.

The cat of extraordinary floof has decided it has received enough attention and has attacked dad's hand with both its claws and sharp teeth.

It releases its death grip on Dad's left hand giving him a judgemental look as it saunters from the room.

Sitting at the table next to Ben, Dad rubs his clawed hand.

"Morning Dad, looks like you found the cat's last nerve!"

Vinnie jokes, referencing that most favourite of adult phrases. Dad smiles wryly at Vinnie as Mum joins them all at the table.

A hush settles, the atmosphere in the room tinged with uncertainty as the two boys look at their parents.

"You know that we love you both very much."

There is a slight pause whilst Mum looks at Dad, he smiles back at the two boys nodding in agreement.

This cannot be good...

Mum lets out a nervous sigh as she continues.

"Well, your Dad and I have not been
getting along well for a long time now..."

Mum stops as if the words are caught in her throat, she looks over at Dad.

"....We have decided it would be best if
we didn't live together anymore.
This means that you will live with Mum
most of the time and we can see each
other at weekends..."

The word 'weekends' came out in a strained choking manner, causing Dad
to stop. He looks over at the two boys.

Vinnie can hear Alfie's words echoing around his head.

Divorce....move
away...new boyfriend....

As he responds to Dad, Vinnie looks over at Ben who has been struck dumb by this unexpected revelation. He can see he is close to tears.

"But why? Where will we go? When will we go?
Am I going to have to get a bus to school?
What about bedtimes, how will we say goodnight
to you?............"

As the avalanche of questions spills from Vinnie's mouth,
the Egolian is going full steam ahead;
worry, blame, fear are coursing through Vinnie's veins.

Mum has managed to regain her composure and even has a smile on her face as she responds to Vinnie.

"I have found us somewhere to move to, not far from here, so no bus will be needed. Dad can phone you whenever he wants, you could say goodnight on a video call during the week."

Vinnie stares at his mum in utter disbelief as he stands from the table and runs from the room. He flys up the stairs two at a time in a bid to seek the sanctuary of his bedroom.

"Vinnie, please come back, let's talk about it...."

He can hear mum calling, but the tears are flowing down his face and his stomach feels like he has been sucker-punched in the solar plexus.

He is struggling to breathe as he enters the room, waves of uncertainty wash over him.

Throwing himself on his bed he cries into his pillow, muffling the sound from anyone in listening distance. The Orb is on top of the wardrobe, it is fully aware of what has just transpired in the kitchen and allows Vinnie some time to process the situation.

As The Orb watches, Vinnie sits up and wipes his nose on the back of his hand which he then rubs on his trousers before closing his eyes.

The Orb watches transfixed as Vinnie finds his 'happy place' inside him. As Vinnie sits, there is a gentle knock at the bedroom door causing Vinnie to open his eyes.

The door opens and Ben walks in with a tear-stained face.

"What are we going to do Vin? I don't want to leave, I don't want to only see Dad sometimes. Vin....."

The last word causes tears to stream from Ben's eyes as he looks at his big brother. There is a fearful troubled look upon Ben's face and his breathing is fast and shallow.

Vinnie recognises this look, in Ben he sees himself.

He sees a previous version of himself.

He sees the scared boy from a week ago.

He knows just what to do.

"Ben, close your eyes."

Ben follows Vinnie's instruction without question, the energy coming off Vinnie is one of love and compassion and Ben can feel this, he just doesn't realise it.

Ben is full of trust and belief in his big brother.

Vinnie looks at his little brother sitting on his bed eyes closed, and he has an immense feeling of protectiveness inside him. He now understands what The Orb meant when choosing to act from a place of fear or love.

Vinnie feels good inside knowing he has the power to help, this causes a smile to form on his lips despite the chaos all around him, he takes a small breath in as he begins.

"Ok, good. Now I want you to breathe in through your nose as if you are sniffing a fart from under your duvet......"

Oh dear, *dear* **Reader** of the words. This is *where* **we** must leave **our** intrepid Hero for *now.*

Such a *long way* **he** has come in just *seven days.*
I suspect that *Egolian* is quaking in its very boots at this *latest* turn of *events.*

Our **Hero** has *received* some *ghastly news,* a week **ago** I *suspect* he would have got *super angry* and thrown his *things around.*
He *most* certainly would **not** have *allowed* his brother into his *bedroom* and would have *definitely not* have sat *him* on the **bed** and consoled **him.**

But *our* **Hero** is much *changed,* his **journey** has *only just* begun *yet* **he** has **learned** *much about* **himself** and the tools to help **him** *along* his **way.**

What an **amazing** *teacher* The Orb is.

It is *said* **Reader,** that 'when the *student* is **ready,** the *teacher* **appears'.**

I *believe* our **Hero** is more than *ready,* **he** is conquering so *much* in such a *short* space of *time.* I **wonder** what his *future* will **hold.**

Reader, you are *also* **ready** to *use* the tools we *have been* shown.

I *feel* greatness *inside* of **you.**

There is a Hero in *all of us*.

As Nick Santonastasso *says*: **Focus on your strengths**.

Rhyme time **Reader**!

Rhyme time......

Our Hero has come so far,
Inner strength makes him a superstar.
Faced with news of a disturbing kind,
He sought the power in his mind.

His brother is full of worry and fears,
They fall down his face in the form of tears.
Our Hero knows just what to do,
For once, he felt that way too.

He takes The Orbs teachings and shares them anew,
The power in his mind he now knows is true.
Let's leave our Hero to comfort his kin,
The notebook lies there, let's take a peek in.

Reader, look you will see,
The Orb has gathered every so neatly.
All the things it shared over this week,
It created a toolbox of useful techniques.

I suspect our Hero's story does not end here,
The Egolian still lurks in his deepest fears.
I wonder what his future holds,
His manner is now much more bold.

Reader, I sense that you too have grown,
The power in YOUR mind you now own.
Exciting and scary times lay ahead,
To be faced with confidence, not dread.

Let us come back at a later date,
I am intrigued to see our Hero's fate.
Will he get his controller back?
Will his parent's get back on track?

The answers we will soon find out,
That's what life is all about.
Go, Reader, embrace all it has to give,
For life is there to live, live, live!

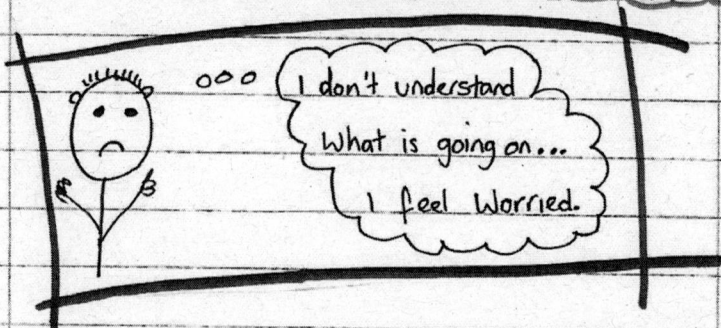

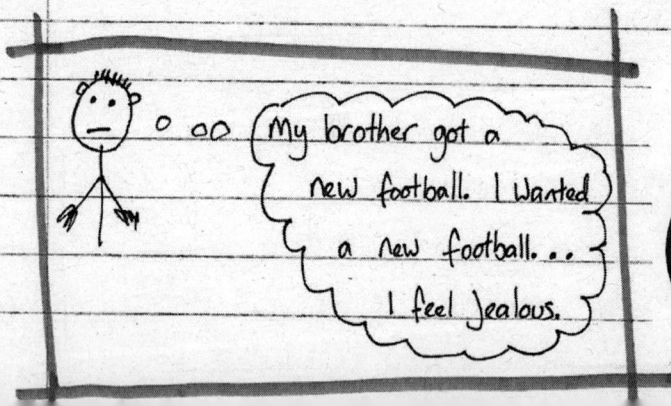

First become aware of the air around you.

feel the air around me.
Can I smell anything?

I am in the 'Now'

Then use your powerful mind to bring the 'Happy Place' back.

Now I feel strong enough to deal with anything!

You can also do things to lift your vibrational energy.

Sing and dance

Play a game

Go Outside

Watch a funny Movie

Remember.. YOU have the power to change YOUR thoughts.

A Hero's Handbook

By The Essence Orb

HERO TOOLKIT

ITEM

SNIFF FART. BLOW BURP TO CALM	SNIFF FART. BLOW BURP FOR ANGER	REIMAGINE YOUR BAD DAY	CALM MONKEY MIND	EXPAND POSITIVE FEELINGS	MAKE EMOTIONS FRIENDS	GETTING IN THE "NOW"	HAPPY PLACE

DO

GET UP EARLY

MAKE YOUR BED

NAME YOUR EGOLIAN

SAY BEDTIME SENTENCE

WRITE GRATITUDE SENTENCE

USE WHAT YOU HAVE

START WHERE YOU ARE

DO WHAT YOU CAN

NAME YOUR EMOTIONS

DO THINGS WHICH MAKE YOU FEEL GOOD

POWER UP

USE EMOTIONAL POWER PACK

WATCH AN INSPIRING OR FUNNY MOVIE

DANCE. LIKE NO ONE IS WATCHING

FOLLOW MOTIVATIONAL PEOPLE ON SOCIAL MEDIA

SMILE

SING FREELY

BELIEVE IN YOURSELF

CHAT WITH A FRIEND

Emotional Powerpack

FULL

Felix
Freedom

Lewys
Love

...nes Joy

Edward
Enthusiastic

| Joy, Freedom, Love |
| Happy, Enthusiastic |
| Positive, Optimistic |
| Content, Hopeful |
| Reflective |
| Frustration, Impatience |
| Worry, Doubt, Disappointment |
| Anger, Blame, Revenge |
| Jealousy, Hatred, Rage |
| Fear, Grief, Depression, Guilt |

Henry
Happy

Ollie
Optimistic

Harvey
Hopeful

Ron
Reflective

Finn
Frustrated

Don
Disappointed

Danny
Doubt

Brian
Blame

Reg Rage

Graham
Guilt

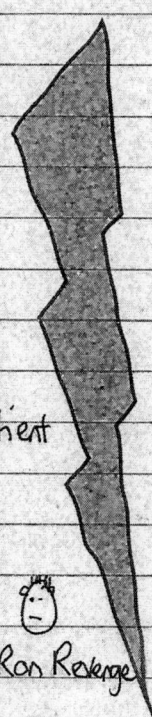

...ositive

...in
...ntent

Impatient

...Worry

...lan

Ron Revenge

Jeremy
Jealousy

...ry
...te

...p

EMPTY

...ar

Greg Grief

Dave Depression

To be Continued....

A Note from the Author.

Once upon a time I believed that I was not good
enough and lived my life feeling less than.
Until one day I realised that I had all the power
I needed inside of me all along.
I finally understood that I could create the life I
dreamed of –   so I did.

And you can too.
            Nicola

            xxx

Gratitude.

A thousand thank you's to my most very favourite Heroes for inspiring me, and making me proud on a daily basis.

Charlie

Stanley

Not forgetting the floofy cat.

Lily

I would also like to thank my husband, Alex Kesaris for always believing in me. My best one Emma Scoones and her tiddlers Ethan and Peyton for filling my heart with joy.

A special thanks to Ashley Malone for being an amazing life coach, Ryan Pinnick for planting the 'Genius' seed, Dr Wayne Dyer and Pam Grout for sharing their awesomeness with the world and Avicii for giving me music to run to.

Credit, where credit is due.

- Photographs used in this book were sourced from:

  www.Pixabay.com

- Music and sound effects used in this book were sourced from:

  www.Zapsplat.com

- QR codes were created using:

  www.qrcode-monkey.com

- Digital drawings by the author were created using:

  https://krita.org

- Videos by the author were created using:

  www.Kizoa.com

- Meditations recorded on:

  www.audacityteam.org

Use these in any of your own creative ideas!

Inspiration Station.

Some of the techniques in this book were
inspired by the teachings of:

Hal Elrod
'The Miracle Morning'
(John Murray Learning)

Esther and Jerry Hicks
'Ask and It Is Given'
(Hay House)

David R Hawkins, M.D., Ph.D.
'Letting Go'
(Hay House)